TENSILE TRADING

TENSILE TRADING

The 10 Essential Stages of Stock Market Mastery

Gatis N. Roze

Grayson D. Roze

WILEY

Published by John Wiley & Sons, Inc., Hoboken, New Jersey.
Published simultaneously in Canada.

For general information on our other products and services or for technical support, please contact our
Customer Care Department within the United States at (800) 762-2974, outside the United States at (317)
572-3993 or fax (317) 572-4002.

Wiley publishes in a variety of print and electronic formats and by print-on-demand. Some material included
with standard print versions of this book may not be included in e-books or in print-on-demand. If this book
refers to media such as a CD or DVD that is not included in the version you purchased, you may download this
material at http://booksupport.wiley.com. For more information about Wiley products, visit www.wiley.com.

Library of Congress Cataloging-in-Publication Data:

Names: Roze, Gatis N. | Roze, Grayson D.
Title: Tensile trading : the 10 essential stages of stock market mastery /
 Gatis N. Roze, Grayson D. Roze.
Description: Hoboken, New Jersey : John Wiley & Sons, Inc., [2016] | Series:
 Wiley trading | Includes index.
Identifiers: LCCN 2015051044 | ISBN 978-1-119-22433-4 (hardback); ISBN 978-1-119-22434-1 (ePDF);
ISBN 978-1-119-22435-8 (ePub); ISBN 978-1-119-22775-5 (obook)
Subjects: LCSH: Investments. | Investment analysis. | Speculation. | BISAC:
 BUSINESS & ECONOMICS / Finance.
Classification: LCC HG4521 .R779 2016 | DDC 332.63/22—dc23 LC record available at
http://lccn.loc.gov/2015051044

10 9 8 7 6 5 4 3 2 1

For Lydia.
What began in your memory comes to life in your honor.

CONTENTS

Listen to what the market is saying about others, not
what others are saying about the market.

—Richard Wyckoff

The legendary Warren Buffett once said, "You only have to do a few things right in your life so long as you don't do too many things wrong." This simple bit of wisdom quite perfectly captures the essence of the book you have in your hands today. Our goal as the authors of *Tensile Trading* is to give you the knowledge and understanding necessary to do more of the right things and fewer of the wrong things as you engage the markets.

Our story is unique in that we are a father-son team sharing the secrets of the insider-structured investment methodology we both use to trade the financial markets. This book's candid details were forged from a father's desire to pass on to his son the skills and knowledge gleaned from 25 years of experience as a full-time trader-investor.

We built our message upon our real-world experiences as two independent investors, not institutional money managers. Instead of professionals advising clients or managing other people's assets, we are individuals who are dedicated to educating other investors. Our unfiltered, brutally honest guidance is structured as a comprehensive 10-stage roadmap that we ourselves have put to use every day (Figure P.1). This book addresses each stage in a separate chapter. This all-encompassing investment system is designed to increase your probabilities for consistently profitable investing. It is our belief and experience that only you will have the greatest level of *passion* for making your assets grow—it's something no adviser or money manager can match. In fact, as an individual investor, you have a surprising number of significant advantages over institutional money managers. We therefore encourage you

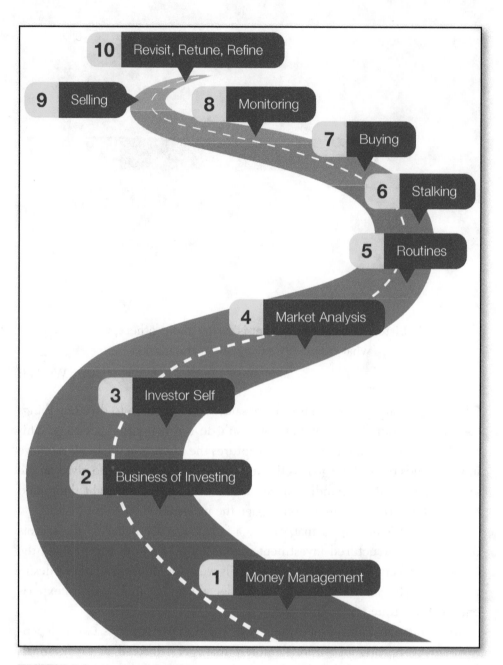

FIGURE P.1 Your Roadmap to Success

not to be seduced by their familiar siren call. They will try to convince you that the game is too complex, too difficult, too time consuming. With the Tensile Trading roadmap before you, their song becomes little more than deceitful persuasion. Trust us, you can do it, you will do it, and we will show you how. We have been amazed to see what people can achieve with discipline and focus, and without the distraction of clients.

Novice investors may marvel at the lengthy preparation period needed to invest successfully—that is, the fact that Tensile Trading addresses six foundational stages before even arriving at the buying stage. More experienced investors, however, will recognize the supreme importance of such preparation and the impact these foundational elements have during the later crucial stages of buying and selling equities. These sorts of high-leverage activities provide the building blocks for a profitable, long-term investment system and are invaluable pieces of your asset growth equation.

The road to successful investing is not an easy one. It has no shortcuts or back roads, despite what some may claim. It is paved with emotional hurdles and will challenge your commitment, but that is precisely why we are here with you. With the detailed direction we provide, the emotional control we encourage, and the disciplined focus we advocate, these obstacles will be little more than speed bumps preceding the freedom of the open road.

■ A Message from Gatis

I have been an active investor since age 16 and a full-time trader since 1989. I have taught investment classes at the postcollegiate level since 2000. One of the most persistent and recurring questions I receive from my circle of fellow traders is "Why do you spend your time teaching?" I was at an investment seminar one year where one of my former students—let's call him James—gave a presentation that unexpectedly provided an answer to this question. This particular student left a high-tech management job to trade the financial markets at just about the same time I began teaching investment courses part-time. As investors who traded only our own accounts, we had, in some sense, been riding the same bus together for quite a few years before this insightful evening.

James recapped the lessons he felt were key to his personal metamorphosis from experimental novice to consistently profitable investor. His presentation stressed the importance of managing emotions, developing a junk information filter, and other valuable bits of wisdom. As I listened to him speak, his words began to offer powerful insights into my motivations as an educator. I realized that I become inspired and energized in the presence of other eager investors like James. Interpersonal interaction pushes me to be a more well-rounded person, while teaching allows me to flex my irreverent attitude and exercise my independent trading personality. For me, the classroom setting turns trading into a team sport of sorts.

I realized during James's talk that I benefit from the variety of investors and students with whom I cross paths because I embrace change and am genetically programmed to be a lifelong learner. With years of classroom experiences to think back on, I am constantly surprised at the education I receive from teaching others. Perhaps not surprisingly, the same has held true during the writing of this book. As you will come to see, I emphasize the importance of review and reflection at every step of the way. In the stock market, looking back at where you have been allows you to see more clearly where you are headed. Writing a book that covers the details of my trading experiences has served this function to a strikingly potent degree. As a result, its words truly are my greatest hits of sorts, carefully refined and remastered.

What I believe makes this book unique is that its words stem from an unusual place in my heart. Approaching normal retirement age, my most significant objective has become to pass down to my son, Grayson, the hard-earned expertise I have accumulated throughout many years of experience trading the markets. This knowledge has become his intellectual inheritance, if you will. It makes me happy to think that my readers can benefit from the same intellectual inheritance that I am proud to pass on to him. This program inculcated in Grayson an understanding and passion for the market, as well as the discipline necessary to implement this investing methodology.

I am thankful for my teaching career because it has provided me with the opportunity to educate and involve Grayson and others in the world of investing that I love so deeply. Where other investors and traders with my track record would not divulge 100 percent of their secrets, I have no such reluctance. Where my own best interests once stood, I now have my son's and students' in their place.

As you read this book, rest assured that I have not simply put together an investment program that I can market to stroke my ego. Instead, I have detailed my comprehensive strategic roadmap and feel proud to share it with you, just as I am proud to teach it to my son. My motivation behind this program's success is largely to create a program that will provide both him and you with the strongest foundation possible for all future investing endeavors.

My son has now graduated from college and developed his own love of the markets, and our work together on this book has evolved into a wonderful collaborative project between us. The teacher has become the student, as he has begun to provide me with his lessons and perceptions gleaned from his own investing experiences. I have an unbending faith in the Tensile Trading program, not only because of my own validation of its principles and my decades of experience from which it is derived, but also because of the amazing metamorphosis that I have witnessed firsthand as my son has enthusiastically and profitably embraced the lessons I have taught him. Based on my own trading results as well as the growth I have seen among the thousands of students I have educated, I am confident that this book and the program it covers will yield similarly satisfying results in your own investing efforts. Good luck, and remember: trade well; trade with discipline!

A Message from Grayson

My first encounter with the stock market came at the young age of 10, when my father printed out a series of price charts and taught me the meaning of trend. With a thick pink highlighter and a basic knowledge of rudimentary price movements, I accompanied him to a number of his investment courses, where I demonstrated my newfound understanding to his students by drawing trend lines on the various charts they would challenge me with. As my participation in these courses became a more regular occurrence, my appreciation for the meaning of these charts, lines, and numbers quickly grew.

By the time I started high school, I was managing a diverse portfolio of stocks, mutual funds, and exchange-traded funds (ETFs) alongside my father. Even at this young age and with a relatively basic level of experience, I was able to trade successfully, thanks to a simple yet effective methodology and an established set of specific routines. These core foundations have been an invaluable element of my investing approach and remain the basis of my trading process today. It is rare to find a teenager who is willing to listen to the advice and tutoring of his father, and I was certainly no exception to that trend. But when it came to the stock market, it was impossible for me to deny the value in his teachings. My belief in this book stems from the impact that the Tensile Trading program has had on my own financial management. I have lived its words and put them to use, and for that reason, I have nothing but confidence in it.

As we've written in these pages, an individual investor never succeeds as a lone wolf. The same certainly can be said of authors in the publishing arena. No successful book is ever written in a vacuum without the collaboration of many key people. There is a long list of colleagues, family, and friends who have participated in the creation of this book. To those who have sustained us throughout this process and guided us in more ways than we can describe, we sincerely thank you from the bottom of our hearts.

Up front, we want to thank the many people at John Wiley & Sons who have worked tirelessly to make it all happen. In particular, we are grateful to Evan Burton for his faith in us and his vision of the project from day one; to Tula Batanchiev for shepherding us through the publishing process and making it a smooth and enjoyable experience; and to Christina Verigan for her unceasing guidance along the way and her superb technical skills bringing this book together at all stages.

Along with our champions at Wiley, we owe special thanks to three other people who were instrumental in the publishing of this book. First, we are grateful to our agent, Ted Bonanno, for his skill and expertise in representing two first-time authors and guiding them with grace and patience. Second, we salute Louisa Diodato, our hometown hero of an editor, who applied such extraordinary copyediting talents to these pages. And, finally, we want to thank Loren O'Laughlin, our graphic designer, for working his creative magic on this book, both inside and out.

Our indebtedness does not end there, however. We owe heartfelt gratitude to Chip Anderson and the entire StockCharts.com team for their truly unending encouragement and inspiration. They are the often unheralded patrons of successful individual investors everywhere, and they deserve much applause. Our hats are off to the two people in our closest family circle who deserve special recognition. First, to our mentor and friend, "Uncle" Harvey Baraban, who has been there every step of the way encouraging us to share our experiences and our message with a wider audience. And our deepest thanks to Jolie Roze, the world's greatest wife and mother, for the many years of unbending love and unconditional support that it took to see this project through from its very earliest gestation.

■ A Special Note from Gatis Roze

At its essence, this book is the result of a number of life passages that occurred for me, starting in the early 1990s as I transitioned from a Silicon Valley career to becoming my own full-time money manager. The initial catalyst for what turned out to be a very successful journey is due in equal parts to the late Paul Ferwerda and Dr. Henry "Hank" Pruden. In 1990, I had the sheer good fortune of hiring Paul Ferwerda to help me open a family money management office in Burlingame, California. He had just retired from Wall Street and was happy to help me get organized. Paul was the founder and first president of the Technical Securities Analysts Association (TSAA), the nation's oldest society devoted to the study and development of stocks and commodities. Paul Ferwerda introduced me to Hank Pruden, a distinguished professor at Gold Gate University, who had also served as the TSAA president and was an early advocate of behavioral finance. It was Dr. Pruden's courses on the Wyckoff investment methods that then launched a serious passion in me for all things relating to the stock market and investing—a passion that is still burning brightly today. I've continued to pass the Pruden-Ferwerda torch to many future generations of investors, including my own son.

I am also grateful to Bruce Fraser, who taught these Wyckoff courses alongside Hank Pruden. It was a unique time and place that attracted a truly extraordinary cadre of investors to their classes at GGU in San Francisco. Fortuitously, I was one of a troupe of stock market technicians who banded together to study for the early Chartered Market Technicians (CMT) certification. I was lucky to have had their enthusiasm and fellowship as we worked to achieve that degree, and I salute each and every one of those early Wyckoffians. A piece of their shared wisdom and inspiration resides within this book.

During my early years as a full-time investor, I was especially blessed to befriend Harvey Baraban, who to this day happily serves as my mentor and devil's advocate in all things concerning life, love, and the markets. When I first met Harvey, he had just retired from Baraban Securities, where he had trained over 30,000 individuals for certification as stockbrokers. With our shared zeal for the markets, we developed a deep and abiding friendship that has spanned the years, no matter what the distance. I owe him a profound debt for challenging me to share my stock market experiences and investment knowledge with others. This book is a direct result of my efforts to meet Harvey's challenge and undertake the teaching of postcollege investment courses.

Teaching investment courses has been an integral part of my own journey as an investor, and I owe a significant debt of gratitude to the circle of students and stock market enthusiasts who have taken my courses over the past 15 years and listened to me preach the trading tenets included in this book. With their spirited dedication, they have made me refine my methodologies and sharpen my communication skills, all the while helping me become a more consistently profitable investor in the process. I am incalculably thankful for their support and their friendship.

Finally, there are two other key individuals who have been instrumental in this personal journey. First, I owe profound thanks to Chip Anderson, the president of StockCharts. I fondly recall sitting in my office with Chip soon after he had started StockCharts.com and talking about his vision for the cloud-based charting website. Being an educator at heart, Chip's passion was not only contagious but was pivotal in my own decision to begin teaching investments. Over the 15 years since that day, Chip has been a valued resource for ideas and a staunch supporter of my own efforts to help individuals become successful investors.

Finally, it might seem somewhat unusual for one coauthor to salute the other coauthor, but it is apropos in this instance. In looking back over my personal investing sojourn, I owe my very deepest thanks to my son and coauthor, Grayson Roze. It was his idea to start this project based on my class syllabus. More important, it was his boundless energy, passion for investing, and writing prowess that produced this book. I am indebted to Grayson for making it happen. I look at him with both wonder and appreciation—thankful that he took such a deep-seated interest in his father's life work from such an unusually early age. His dedication to our partnership in writing this book has been an extraordinary gift from a son to his proud father.

Gatis N. Roze is a veteran full-time stock market investor who has traded his own account since 1989 unburdened by the distraction of clients. He holds an MBA from the Stanford Graduate School of Business, is a Chartered Market Technician (CMT), and is a past president of the Technical Securities Analysts Association (TSAA). After several successful entrepreneurial ventures, he retired in his early 40s to focus on investing in the financial markets. With consistent success as a stock market trader, he began teaching investments at the postcollege level in 2000 and continues to do so today. A renowned communicator, he has taught thousands of investors in sold-out seminars for the American Association of Individual Investors (AAII), the Market Technicians Association (MTA), Bellevue College, and StockCharts University. He also writes the popular blog the *Traders Journal*, which has a global following and appears weekly at StockCharts.com.

■ ■ ■

Grayson D. Roze has worked in the financial services industry for StockCharts.com since 2012. He now serves as a business manager at the company. Grayson holds a bachelor's degree from Swarthmore College, where he studied economics and psychology. At a young age, he began pursuing his interest in the financial markets by attending investment classes and starting to trade under the guidance of his father. At the age of 18, Grayson began investing his own account and has since become an accomplished trader in his own right. *Tensile Trading* was his vision as a vehicle to lay out his father's investment wisdom and convey it to a wider audience.

Money Management

Think of your future in the market as a road trip. Your journey does not start 50 miles down the street; rather, it begins at home when you choose your destination, spread out the map on the kitchen table, and carefully plan the route for your upcoming adventure, keeping the big picture in mind. Proper money management is the mapping stage of your road trip. Before you pull onto the investing highway, you must thoroughly determine your personal financial position, truthfully establish your investment goals and motivations, and develop a deep understanding of how to advance from where you are today. So what exactly is *money management*? Frustrated with the absence of one agreed-upon definition within the financial world, I polled more than 80 investors throughout my classes—a combination of continuing education classes, daylong seminars, and multiweek sessions—to see what we could come up with. Collectively, we created the following comprehensive definition, which encompasses all that is necessary for a proper and effective money management plan:

> First and foremost, money management is an ongoing process. More descriptively, it is a documented, personally appropriate financial framework that describes the types of investments and strategies you feel will align best with your personal goals, objectives, and priorities. These guidelines describe the rules and tools you deem appropriate in managing your wealth. They acknowledge your risk tolerance and the risk management techniques you employ to protect your assets. Finally, they provide an ever-changing, lifelong timeline and roadmap recording the methodologies and resources you use to ensure disciplined stewardship of your assets as you attempt to maximize the return on your investments.

As an educator, my objective is to equip you with the tools and skills necessary for you to become profitable as an investor and consistently replicate that profitability. Ultimately, these should be your goals, too. Your aim as an investor should be to make the right preparations and the wisest decisions to move the probabilities in your favor and become consistently profitable, and creating a detailed money management plan is the first step toward this goal. It is all about:

1. Knowing what you have,
2. Knowing how to protect it,
3. Knowing how to grow it, and
4. Writing it out in a personalized investment plan.

Too frequently, novice investors display a harmful overeagerness by choosing to jump in head first to step 3—growing your assets—while ignoring steps 1, 2, and 4. Buying a stock may be the most flashy and exciting of our four elements, but to pursue this item first is to kill your odds of success and lower your probability of making money on a consistent basis. Only after you've completed the first three steps (Figure 1.1) and written it out into a clear, actionable plan are you ready to actually jump into the market.

The first task—in reaching any goal—is to lay a solid foundation. You must start with the basics and work your way up. At the most fundamental level, this means you must learn to speak the language of the market. Every profession—from medicine to engineering to accounting to law—has its own unique vocabulary, and the stock market is certainly no exception. For example, knowing the difference between a market order and limit order could be the difference between a profitable trade and a losing trade. There is an extensive collection of glossaries and resources online that help explain the investment language. Find the one that works for you, and refer back to it frequently.

In addition, you must take the time to learn the structure of the market. For example, Dow Jones, Standard & Poor's (S&P), and the Frank Russell Company all create unique indexes or groupings of equities. They are then paid a licensing fee by users of their indexes. Understand that while these indexes may appear different, all three companies are slicing and dicing the exact same total market made up of the exact same stocks (Figure 1.2). Because the equities

FIGURE 1.1　Three Steps: Asset Creation, Asset Protection, Asset Growth

that constitute them are all the same, this means that the Dow Jones Industrial Average is a subset of the S&P 500 index, which in turn is a subset of the Russell 3000. Taking the time to properly educate yourself will prevent you from being confused by all this slicing and dicing and will serve you tremendously as you move forward through your investing career. Think of education as a prerequisite and a critical part of building your foundation because choosing to learn on the fly can quickly become a very expensive decision.

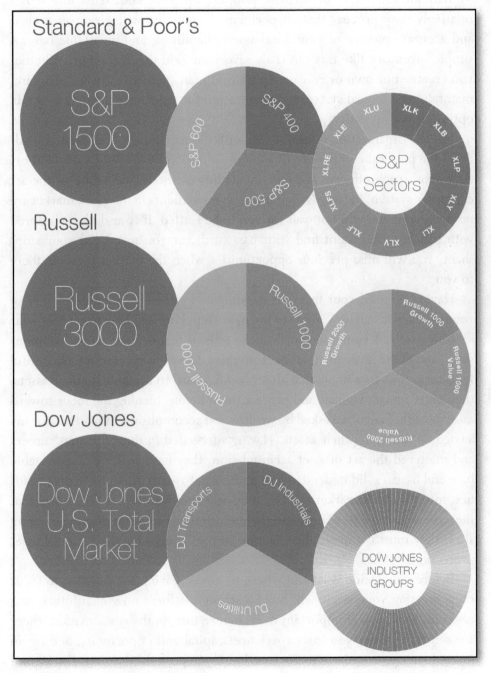

FIGURE 1.2   Market Index Pies

Let us address the first point in creating a detailed money management plan: knowing what you have. Before you can pass go and collect $200—even before you can set your piece down on the board to play the game—it is imperative that you thoroughly sort through your personal financial data to understand exactly what assets you own and where they are invested.

To do this, I update my net worth statement on an annual basis every January, and even in this short time frame, there is not a year that goes by without some sort of surprise popping up. That said, trust me: It is a relatively easy process that, if performed annually, will give you a clear and accurate picture of your total assets, liabilities, and investable base. A simple inventory like this can truly save your skin down the line. Whether you create your own or rely on a portfolio management software program, maintaining a logical system of organization for your financial data is not an option; it is a necessity.

But the organization does not end with the paperwork. You must also address the physical component of your organization by keeping a tidy and orderly workspace, efficient and functional filing methods, and a state-of-the-art computer system. In today's digital world, movements in the stock market are instantaneous and will not wait for you to be settled. If your desk is cluttered with papers, you cannot find your passwords, or you misplaced your stops sheet, you will miss precious opportunities when the market presents them to you.

Having assessed your financial standing and gained an accurate picture of your assets, you can now move to the next step: knowing how to protect your existing assets. A common sports cliché tells us that defense wins championships, and in the investment arena, a premier defense is paramount. Successful long-term investors know that after working hard to accumulate their assets, they must remain vigilant and protect them before turning the focus toward asset growth. I am often asked by wealthy and accomplished individuals for my advice on managing their assets. Having succeeded in their previous careers and mastered the art of asset accumulation, they have built up an investable base and have a solid understanding of their net worth. Anxious to dive head-first into the stock market and begin buying equities, they fail to realize that they are skipping a step. I explain that before they can jump into the exciting stuff, they must complete the essential step of addressing the basics of asset protection.

Before you decide what and where to invest, having the patience to focus on protecting your assets will build a strong platform on which future success can develop. It is important to recognize that, in the stock market, there are only two losses you can experience: capital and opportunity. Seizing an investment opportunity is important, but if you push the envelope too far and fail to protect your capital, these opportunities will no longer be available to you in the future. If you protect your capital, however, there will always be another opportunity. As such, protecting your assets must remain of prime importance.

Start your protection plan with a thorough review of the basics, such as insurance, estate planning, identity theft protection, professionally advised tax strategies, and secure record keeping. Find a competent estate attorney, keep your will up to date, and review it every two years. Make sure you have proper asset coverage, medical insurance, and liability insurance. Be prudent in protecting your personal information by using shredders and secure mailboxes. Devise proper password protocols, and hire a firm to monitor your credit agency accounts. Install software to inventory all your assets and reconcile your net worth annually. Seek the help of a good tax accountant to help minimize your tax payments. Set yourself up for success by ensuring these items are taken care of before you begin investing. Your future self will thank you for it.

It may sound somewhat self-evident, but paying off your debts and minimizing your liabilities is part and parcel of prudent asset management. We can debate the appropriateness of using leverage, but suffice it to say my position is to steer clear of this strategy. It has been my observation that debt and leverage make poor partners with wise investment decisions. On a personal note, I am an advocate of developing a savings attitude by learning to live on a specific percentage of what you earn while investing the balance. In my experience, even teaching your kids about money and the value of effective management can be part of your own money management plan. (You will be surprised by what you yourself learn in the process!) With these items in line, you will be on your way to a secure and well-protected asset base you can then grow comfortably, confidently, and consistently.

■ Crafting Your Money Management Plan

As you set out on your investing journey, the foundation you lay by carefully assessing, organizing, and managing your assets will become your secret for future success in the market, giving you an edge that all investors need but few truly have. Attempting to invest without a detailed and accurate money management plan is like trying to nail Jell-O to a wall: impossible. Creating this personal plan is imperative; it will help you remain in control of not only your investing but also your financial well-being as a whole. Your plan should include the following seven characteristics:

1. Based on a very personal and appropriate financial framework document.
2. Exists in writing.
3. Thoroughly describes your goals, objectives, and priorities.

4. Outlines your investment methodology and strategies.
5. Describes your trading tools and sets money management rules to help you remain consistent and focused.
6. Acknowledges your individual risk tolerance and describes the risk management techniques you will employ to protect your assets.
7. Updated on a regular basis.

Personal and Appropriate

In order to be successful, your plan must be based on a very personal and appropriate financial framework document. There is no one-size-fits-all approach, so you need to customize your plan to account for your existing assets, financial goals, risk tolerance, strategic preferences, and your stage in life—among other factors. This list is by no means exhaustive.

Your assets are yours alone, and they must be organized and managed according to what feels most appropriate for you.

Put It in Writing

Too often, people make the mistake of overestimating their abilities and believing they can keep track of everything in their head. Furthermore, a written document is a communication vehicle for sharing and validating your intentions with your significant other, your family, and any outside attorneys or accountants you may involve. Taking the time to write out your money management plan and put everything on paper is the most effective way to not only stay organized and accurate with your financial data but also be brutally honest with yourself about your financial reality. If your asset management plan is committed only to memory, it is easy to bend the numbers and convince yourself that pouring another $10,000 into a stock cannot hurt. But if this plan is written down, it may be obvious that another $10,000 is not prudent. Keeping your finances on paper introduces a level of precision and responsibility to your financial data that is more difficult to twist, helping to ensure that you are honest with yourself in your investment decisions.

Thorough and Descriptive

Your money management plan thoroughly describes your goals, objectives, and priorities.

This is a wonderful opportunity for you to reflect on where you are financially and where you would like to be moving forward. Again, it is vital that you be honest and realistic with yourself. If your goal is a 40 percent return in your first year, you may want to think again. Start smaller, and work your way up to bigger, better, more ambitious objectives as your level of experience grows. Shortcuts are not an option, so be diligent and don't rush.

Methodology and Strategies

Your plan also outlines your investment methodology and strategies. Like the other parts of your plan, it's important that this be written down.

Detailing exactly how you intend to invest your money and the strategies you will use to grow your assets is a critical step toward successful investing. Without a specific and focused methodology, your investing will lack direction and consistency. Note, too, that your methodology and the strategies you use to support it will evolve over time and may take years to fully develop; this is all part of the investing game. Writing out a methodology now will start you off on the right path, and by embracing good habits, you will ensure a successful future for yourself in the stock market. We will cover the steps of constructing your methodology in later stages, but it is important to understand now that it is a living document that will be adjusted on an ongoing basis to reflect your personal growth as an investor.

Trading Tools and Money Management Rules

As your plan expresses your goals, it also addresses how to get there. It describes your trading tools and sets money management rules to help you remain consistent and focused.

In today's age of Internet overload, there are thousands of resources marketed as investment aids. By carefully filtering through these, choosing the handful that are right for you, and intimately familiarizing yourself with them, you will increase your efficiency and effectiveness as a trader. Note that for our purposes in this book, the terms *investor* and *trader* can generally be used interchangeably. This reflects the idea that each and every investor must identify the trading time frame that best suits his or her own temperament, goals, and priorities. In the larger context, investors tend to hold their equities for longer periods, while traders lean toward shorter periods. For us, this distinction is not important. What is important, however, is for you to identify and fully commit to the time frame you are most comfortable with. Make this a rule for yourself, and document it in your money management plan.

As you begin to invest in the market, a firm set of rules will become your guide to turn trades into profit. Using a tiered ladder system, for example, both when buying into a position and when selling out of a position, will add structure to your investment strategies. Numerous academic studies have shown this yields superior returns in the long run. If you are planning a total investment of $10,000 in a specific equity, first buy 20 to 30 percent of that sum as a feeler for the investment. If the markets validate this first position and it shows a profit, buy another 20 to 30 percent, and continue to monitor the position. When both your first and second positions are profitable, buy the balance of the $10,000 total investment. The same structure applies on the sell side of the coin, modified slightly to reflect the fact that markets move down much faster than they trend up. Your first sell could be up to 50 percent of the position, your second sell could be 30 to 50 percent of the position, and your third sell should be the remainder.

In addition, set stops on your investments to avoid excessive risk and protect your precious capital. In a later stage, we will discuss in detail the mechanics of setting stops, but it is important to note here that whether you use hard stops (entered in the market) or soft stops (kept on your own desktop), this asset protection tool is indispensable. After a 25 percent run-up or higher in the price of the equity, your methodology should call for you to tighten your stops, locking in profits and avoiding the loss of a profitable trade. You must learn to listen carefully to what the market is telling you. Respect its power and stay consistent by monitoring your positions closely. This simple handful of rules has been my savior time and time again, and my strict adherence to them has made me a successful, profitable investor.

Risk Tolerance and Protection Strategies

In order for you to be successful, your plan must acknowledge your individual risk tolerance and describe the risk management techniques you will employ to protect your assets.

Always remember that without capital, there will be no market opportunities. Everyone has a different level of risk he or she can handle, both emotionally and financially. Understanding your personal risk tolerance is crucial to understanding yourself as an investor and aligning your decisions with your methodology in a manner appropriate for the current market landscape.

Updated Regularly

Your management plan is updated on a regular basis.

This is vital. Whether you do this every month, every six months, or once a year, find what works for you and stick to it. Your assets are constantly shifting, particularly as their growth becomes a more important part of your equation. This means you must routinely revisit your money management plan to reevaluate your goals, reassess your priorities, and refine your investment methodology as you continue to mature as an investor.

Taking a proactive, hands-on approach to writing your investment plan is the first step toward building a solid foundation for successful investing.

Writing out your plan, however, is only half the battle. Actually believing it and staying true to your words is the other essential half.

As you begin to put this plan to use and develop your investment methodology, you must truly embrace and understand the law of probabilities. Despite what so many market pundits claim, nothing is ever 100 percent certain—but making the proper preparations, formulating the right decisions, and remaining focused on your goals and objectives as written in your money management plan will put the wind at your back and increase your probability of consistently profitable trades.

Personally, I know that my beliefs in four crucial areas determine how my trading profits will stack up at the end of the year. I regularly ask myself the following four questions:

- Do I still believe 100 percent in my methodology as I have written it in my trading plan?

- Do I still have control of my emotions, and am I still displaying the appropriate behavior necessary to trade the markets successfully?

- Is my trust in my tools and indicators unwavering such that I can and will confidently risk my capital based on their readings?

- Do I still believe in the law of probabilities and have faith that by executing my system with consistency I will earn a profit?

In answering and embracing these four questions, I see myself as a trapeze artist, able to let go of the bar and trust that my partner will be there to catch me. In this sense, my beliefs become my trading partner. The bottom line is that as an investor, you must be intimately in tune with your beliefs, goals, and priorities at all times, and you must be aware of any indications that might suggest your faith in them is drifting off course. Understanding your own beliefs about the stock market and investing will empower you to produce consistent profits in a manner no other personal attribute can do.

Becoming a Successful Investor

At the most basic level, there are three central elements to becoming a successful investor. We have already covered the first: writing out your trading plan. Having a trading plan that is realistic, current, and actionable is essential as you strive to meet your investment goals. Personalized and adjusted over time to reflect changes in your life, the plan and methodology that you set out for yourself will increase your probability of success. After writing out your plan, you must put it to use and take action, which is our second element in becoming a successful investor.

On both the buying and selling ends of an investment, taking action is one of the toughest hurdles for budding investors to overcome. Too often, I see students let opportunities slip through their fingers because they are scared to put the hammer down and buy that stock. More tragically, I see students who have no fears about buying, but freeze up and become incapable of pulling the trigger when it comes time to sell. As the stock price continues to fall, this becomes a very, very expensive decision. Strangely, people often classify no action as the absence of decision making. But don't be fooled: Failing to pull the trigger is a decision in itself, and an incorrect one at that. When the markets are telling you that you are wrong, you must do everything you can to stop being wrong. In the scenarios above, these investors are making the wrong decisions, and the only way to fix the problem and turn the situation around is to take action.

With the proper preparations in place, you must believe in your methodology and have faith in yourself so you can go out and make it happen. Acting now beats waiting, because the more you wait, the more daunting that action will appear in the future. To help calm any concerns and make that hurdle just a little bit shorter to jump over, select the risk-to-reward profile that allows you to sleep comfortably at night without excessive worry. Broadly diversify your portfolio to limit your exposure, and take on riskier positions in only small portions. Depending on your risk tolerance, index funds, exchange-traded funds (ETFs), and mutual funds may be more appropriate for you than individual stocks. Finding the right balance between these investment vehicles and applying the principles of your trading plan is a crucial step toward getting you out of the locker room and onto the playing field.

The third element of becoming a successful investor is a theme I cannot stress enough: staying focused and disciplined. This is where the work you put into crafting your detailed money management plan will pay off. You have laid out your goals, objectives, and priorities and put them down in writing, and as you begin to invest, you must keep these in sight at all times. It is tempting to deviate from them in favor of short-term performance, but the impulsive decision to do so can prove costly in the long run and will steer you away from becoming the consistent, long-term investor that you know you can become.

Using benchmarks specific to your goals and priorities, such as the Russell 3000, to evaluate your performance will help you stay on the proper course. Just like your routine trips to the doctor's office, regular checkups and comparisons between your investment history and your money management plan will keep your portfolio healthy and your profits consistent. Most important, find ways to keep your investing fun and interesting—a hobby, if you will— rather than a burden or a source of stress. The global markets today allow you to trade 24 hours a day if you are so inclined, an unrealistic figure for even the most experienced of investors. By deciding exactly how much time you are willing and able to devote to the stock market, you will feel more directed in your time management and be more effective during the time you do spend focusing on your investing.

For me, thinking of the stock market and my trading as a constant source of education has helped me remain positive and continuously passionate about my investing. I view losing trades as my way of paying tuition to the market, just as I did in college and graduate school. When I experience a loss in the market, I examine the experience and focus not on the immediate frustration of losing money but on the lessons the trade has taught me and the mistakes I made that I will correct in the future. This is a constructive method of personal growth that will help pull your head out of the past and turn your attention toward the future. Finding your own secret formula for making your investing perpetually engaging will keep your outlook positive, help you stay persistent in your trading, and prove profitable in the long run.

■ The Importance of Asset Allocation

Without exception, every one of the world's most powerful corporations devotes a large staff and hires expensive consultants each year to maintain its corporate strategic plan. An extension of the initial business plan, this annually updated document analyzes the competitive landscape, details current cost structures and sales channels, and explains how the company plans to outmaneuver its competitors on the battlefield of commerce. This process of methodically preparing and strategizing before continuing on with full operations is an essential element of any successful business.

As an investor, you must subscribe to a very similar concept of strategic planning. The equivalent of your own personal business plan is what we will refer to as your personal asset allocation profile. There is an endless array of puzzles you will need to solve throughout your investment journey, but none is more crucial than carefully and methodically crafting your own asset allocation plan.

Far too often, new, overeager investors commit the exact same classic mistake by ignoring this pivotal step. Rather than first looking in the mirror and asking what types of assets suit them best both intellectually and emotionally, they dive headfirst into the market—any market—without hesitation. Predictably, the markets quickly deem these impatient investors unworthy. After suffering the harsh realities of their careless urgency, they are eventually shamed into deep personal reflection and forced to ask the important questions they failed to consider before they began. These individuals learn the hard way that it is unavoidably critical to outline your goals, objectives, and expectations well before committing serious money to the financial markets

and placing any actual trades. This is the central theme of strategic asset allocation. Before moving forward, consider the following definition, which we've
created for the purposes of Tensile Trading:

> For an individual investor, asset allocation can be defined as the strategic
> selection and assembly of a diversified assortment of financial assets with
> prudent correlation values in appropriate percentage weights that reflect
> the investor's personal risk tolerance balanced against his or her profit
> expectations, investment timeline, and other unique financial goals that
> the investor wishes to achieve.

At its core, asset allocation hinges on diversification. This alone is nothing
revolutionary; diversification has been a central component of basic investment principles for many generations. You do not need a doctorate or a master's in business administration to recognize that putting all your eggs in one
basket is a foolish investment plan doomed only to fail. The classic diversification model is most commonly represented as a pie chart split into four pieces
(Figure 1.3). According to this model, invested capital should be divided between four broad asset classes to reduce a portfolio's exposure to downside
risk throughout all phases of the business cycle.

As time has worn on and financial markets throughout the world have ex-
panded, however, diversification models have become much more complex.
Economists, mathematicians, and financial professionals have shown that utilizing more sophisticated models of diversified asset allocation can reduce risk
still further while also potentially increasing total returns. In fact, diversification has become so widely embraced that in 1974, the government enacted
federal Employee Retirement Income Security Act (ERISA) laws that established minimum standards for asset allocations in pension plans and required

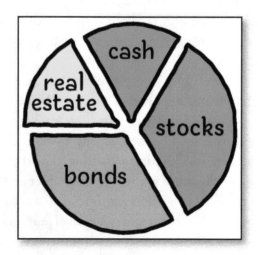

FIGURE 1.3 Elementary Diversification Model

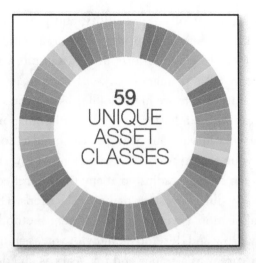

FIGURE 1.4   Tensile Trading's Modern Diversification Model

compliance by portfolio managers. What this means is that the elementary diversification pie we previously sliced into four large asset classes is no longer representative of the investable landscape available to us (Figure 1.4). Instead, the pie has fragmented, giving us dozens more asset classes across which we can allocate our capital.

While the exact number of potential asset groups remains a topic of debate, my eyes have sliced the pie into a collection of 59 unique asset classes across which an investor can diversify his or her portfolio. What is perhaps most important to recognize here is that investing in the modern era is a game of endless choice. In the past few decades, the financial markets throughout the world have played host to unbelievable growth and innovation. Increased globalization, significant expansion of numerous emerging markets, and rapid technological developments have put the entire world only a click away, while the rise of ETFs has brought even more investment options to the table. For a long list of reasons, it is simply impossible for one individual investor in today's global markets to fully understand and analyze all of the economic influences, fundamental inputs, and political motivations that affect financial market prices across all asset classes. The basic reality is that the skill set it takes to manage high-yield bonds in Asia is very different from that required to trade small-cap equities in the United States, for example. As an investor in the twenty-first century, your job is no longer to find the best, most promising assets the markets have to offer in each asset class. There are simply too many options across too many asset groups for this to be even a remotely feasible task. Instead, it is your job as an investor to assemble a specific collection of the best, most promising asset classes that fit your own investor self.

Fortunately, there is an upside to the myriad investment vehicles available across dozens of asset groups: Such a broad array of options allows you to dial in the precise amount of risk, volatility, and performance expectations that you as an investor deem appropriate for your specific personality, financial goals, involvement level, and more. If, for example, your objective is for investing to serve as your primary source of income, your asset allocation profile can be tilted toward more high-yielding asset groups. If you are fearful of inflation, you can invest a larger percentage of your portfolio in, say, real estate ETFs. If low volatility is your goal, you can build a more risk-averse profile by allocating your capital toward more defensive investments. Moreover, these parameters can be easily adjusted at any time to reflect changing liquidity needs, a new schedule, or estate planning decisions. The key here is that embracing asset allocation as your core investment methodology allows your portfolio to safely grow and develop along with you as an investor over time.

From both my career as a trader and my years as an educator, I would be willing to wager that, overall, individuals who focus diligently on asset allocation will outperform their simple stock-picker brethren and achieve far superior financial results in the long run. Moreover, they do so with lower volatility, smaller drawdowns, and much less stress. Any honest financial professional will tell you that it is nearly impossible for individual investors to consistently beat the market by managing a portfolio of exclusively handpicked individual stocks. This system lacks the structure and organization key to consistently returning a solid profit in today's massive globalized marketplace. Focusing primarily on asset allocation, however, puts the long-term odds much more in your favor while still allowing for some degree of hands-on, active management. I see it as the best of both worlds. By identifying the asset groups that are most tailored to your investing style and selecting the best investment vehicles in each respective group—be they ETFs, mutual funds, or your own active management—you narrow your focus from the infinite universe of individual equities to a much more manageable collection of specific assets.

I have always been both intrigued and impressed by the financial management records of many colleges and universities, and I have found that there are valuable insights to be gleaned by analyzing the strategies employed by these schools. Universities such as Harvard, for example, have been able to outperform the S&P 500 over the past few decades by margins that would shock you. Give it a quick search online, and you will see for yourself. What is most interesting to me is that, with multibillion-dollar endowments to manage, the financial experts at these powerful institutions choose to focus diligently on asset allocation. Part of what makes this strategy so effective is that universities prioritize capital preservation ahead of capital growth. The objective of managing a college endowment is to design a portfolio with very low risk and very low volatility. Over a longer period, this allows the endowment to grow at a modest and consistent pace with little risk of falling in value. Such a goal is achieved most successfully through healthy diversification, which helps calm the extremes in all phases of the business cycle. Adopting this as a core financial objective of your own will have tremendous benefits in the long run, preserving the capital you have earned while still allowing it to grow for the future.

◼ Constructing Your Personal Asset Allocation Profile

In the financial industry, the confusing reality is that the exact same terminology is often used to describe quite separate concepts, processes, and subjects. Asset allocation is one of those multifaceted terms. There are a host of subdisciplines within the broader concept of asset allocation, each differing in terms of the investment strategies it employs, the timing mechanisms it uses, and more. Two of these disciplines in particular stand out as the most common: strategic asset allocation and tactical asset allocation.

Strategic asset allocation is the process of creating a personalized portfolio that invests in a diversified mix of asset classes in specific, predetermined percentage weights. The key to strategic asset allocation is that the proportional representation of each asset class within the portfolio is determined by the investor's own risk and return objectives and the time frame according to which he or she plans to invest. Generally, once these parameters are set, the only remaining responsibility in the future is to periodically rebalance the percentage weights of each asset class in the portfolio to maintain the predetermined and desired proportional representations.

Tactical asset allocation, on the other hand, essentially begins with a strategic asset allocation portfolio and then regularly adjusts the individual proportions of each of the asset classes up or down to reflect current market conditions. The intention of this method is to continually overweight high-performing assets and underweight poor-performing assets, thereby more effectively timing investments to boost returns.

This brief background of these two common asset allocation concepts is important because the Tensile Trading asset allocation methodology—that is, the methodology we cover in this book—is a hybrid of both the strategic and tactical strategies. A primary intention of this modification is to capture the benefits of diversification while also accommodating most investors' desire to actively manage at least some portion of their portfolio themselves or implement some type of individual equity trading strategy. It can be a challenge to feel fulfilled by spending your time simply allocating capital across different funds and rebalancing portfolio weights. The reality is that, while immensely important, these tasks sometimes lack the excitement many individuals are looking for in the markets. The Tensile Trading approach proudly acknowledges the hands-on nature of the typical individual investor. Instead of denying or minimizing such a tendency, this methodology seeks to harness it in the most constructive and impactful way possible, using what is known as a core-and-explore approach.

Core and Explore

Imagine two categories within your portfolio: core and explore. The core reflects the asset groups you have chosen to form your asset allocation profile. It consists of low-cost, broad-based index funds, ETFs, and mutual funds, widely diversified with proper correlations and limited risk. Your core positions are allocated not only domestically but also globally, and they should weight allocation percentages across an extensive spectrum of asset classes. Broad market allocation is the objective here, and your core should be constructed with the intention of protecting the assets you have accumulated and "staying rich."

With the core settled and invested, you are free to turn your focus to the explore portion of your portfolio. Extending into the explore territory is a gradual and careful process. As a novice, 100 percent of your portfolio should be invested in core positions. As your knowledge grows, your experience level increases, or your investment objectives change, you can slowly begin to shift a small portion of your portfolio into more aggressive explore positions, such as individual stocks, actively managing and trading this segment yourself. This allows you to pursue your capital growth objectives while ensuring that the bulk of your portfolio remains secure in the core. As your success rate expands and you learn from your experiences, you can extend your explore positions from 5 to 10 to 15 percent of your portfolio, all the while maintaining a solid base in your core positions.

The core-and-explore investment strategy is a tried-and-true method of simultaneously protecting and growing your assets. Exercising control and finding the proper balance between asset protection and asset growth by implementing the core-and-explore methodology is an important step toward joining the ranks of consistently successful investors.

Minimizing Costs

Let us pause here for a moment and address the important topic of costs. As an investor, I am a profit maximizer. Costs are counterproductive to this mission and are therefore one of my main hot buttons. Unfortunately, many new investors underappreciate the immense impact costs can have on their returns. Let us assume that, hypothetically, both you and your twin brother start investing $1 million at age 45. Your brother is frugal and pays 1 percent per year in fees. You are less careful and pay 2 percent a year in commissions and fees. Assuming a steady, conservative 3.5 percent rate of return over the next 40 years, your brother's portfolio will have grown in value to $2.7 million—a staggering 50 percent greater than the $1.8 million your otherwise-identical portfolio is now worth. It is simple: fees and expenses matter.

There are the obvious expenses to avoid, such as loaded mutual funds and complex ETFs with high costs, low trading volumes, and wide bid-ask spreads. The less visible fees, though, can be quite ingenious. As an example, for a number of years I owned a mutual fund that is offered to investors in five different variations, each with its own ticker symbol. These separate variations of the exact same fund represent five different configurations of front loads, deferred loads, expense ratios, and 12b-1 fees. To circumvent this institutional trickery, resources such as investment research giant Morningstar (www.morningstar.com) can be critically useful. Morningstar breaks down all the available variations for any mutual fund, allowing you to compare and contrast your options. When faced with this sort of choice, always go for the lowest-cost offering.

ETFs are very much the same. It is common to find multiple ETFs that offer exposure to exactly the same market segment. As a result, none of the funds will provide any sort of meaningful performance advantage over the others. The only conceivable difference between them is the expenses they charge. So before you invest, it is crucial that you take these cost differences into consideration. Over time, this sort of investigative effort and careful decision making will prove its worth many times over.

Fortunately, asset allocation by nature generates fewer transactions than many other investment methodologies. While this may sound trivial at first, every transaction is accompanied by fees and expenses and triggers capital gains taxes that decrease profits. Reducing the number of transactions means more of your money remains just that: yours.

Asset Group Selection

In my own portfolio construction, I have chosen 20 asset groups in which to invest, the vast majority of which represent my portfolio's core. These groups have not been chosen at random; they are specific to my own investing personality. After decades of trading, I know myself well and have carefully selected the assets that best fit my investor self. Most important, by limiting the size of my portfolio to 20 asset classes, I restrict the complexity of my investing process. Together, these 20 asset groups form my asset allocation profile. As I have said before, your asset allocation profile is an extremely personal piece of your investing puzzle. I can provide you with the foundation, but it is ultimately your responsibility to build the house that suits you best.

In my own experience, allocating my capital across a collection of 20 asset groups seems to be my magic number, providing the level of statistical diversification my investor self demands. This spread has allowed me to sail through the turndowns of 1987, 2001, and 2008, for example. I recognize, however, that choosing a personalized collection of 20 asset groups across which to diversify your portfolio may seem like a daunting task for a new investor. I will not claim that 20 is the correct number for everyone; as with so many other elements of successful investing, you must carefully find what works best for you. Perhaps a selection of 10 asset groups provides a more suitable and manageable diversified portfolio. Maybe 20 is not enough, and you must cast an even wider net across 30 asset groups. These are the questions that only time and experience can truly answer. As you develop your own asset allocation profile, I encourage you to explore and experiment.

After you have determined the collection of specific asset groups that will comprise your asset allocation profile, the next step is to decide how best to invest in each of them. For some of these categories, passively managed ETFs may be your strongest option. In others, however, you may find that a specific mutual fund manager has been able to consistently beat a benchmark while investing in that particular asset class. In this case, a mutual fund may the right choice. For each asset group in your allocation profile, your job is to carefully sift through the available options to find the investment vehicle that combines proven performance with affordable costs. This process of determining the strongest, most promising investment option in each specific asset class fosters what I like to refer to as "niche dominance." It ensures that for each asset group you own, your money is invested by the very best of the best, be it in a passive ETF or an actively managed mutual fund.

As I mentioned, my own asset allocation profile consists of 20 asset classes that I have handpicked as most appropriate for the character of my investor self. Of those 20 baskets, I invest in 19 of them using ETFs or mutual funds, passing the management baton to others with the most talent in a particular market segment. I have chosen to actively manage the one remaining asset basket, which is large-cap U.S. growth stocks, myself, generally trading about 10 positions at a time within this asset class.

This constitutes the explore portion of my portfolio. On a daily basis, I am able to trade this basket with a hawk-like focus and overweight the attention I devote to its management. This is made possible only because the time and effort I previously spent carefully setting up the other 19 baskets in my asset allocation profile gives me the confidence to let the capital invested in them grow on its own. I have delegated the responsibility for these other 19 baskets to the professional fund managers or the ETFs who have proven themselves the best of the best in their respective asset classes. I am thereby free to simply supervise from a responsible distance and rebalance my capital allocations as needed.

From experience, I know I can successfully monitor 19 asset baskets and actively manage the 10 individual equities in my U.S. growth stocks basket. This self-awareness is crucial. I acknowledge that I am not Warren Buffett. His intellectual bandwidth could allow him to handle a much more extensive asset allocation profile. This is where brutal honesty about yourself is required. The unfortunate truth is that basic human nature works against you as an investor, always coaxing you to trade outside your boundaries. I have regimented myself to stay within my fence line and not venture outside my established comfort zone, even when the forces of temptation pull strongly. In doing so, I am able to oversee all 20 of my asset baskets and make the appropriate allocation adjustments necessary to limit risk, maximize returns, and sleep peacefully.

Asset Allocation Resources

For newer investors in the process of assembling their own asset allocation profile, there are three key resources that, collectively, help condense the market down into an easily accessible format. Taken together, these resources will allow you to compile a thorough list of currently available mutual funds and ETFs across all asset groups, giving you a logical array of options to consider for each. First, the American Association of Individual Investors (AAII) has an annual guide to the top mutual funds. Focus on AAII's groupings, not necessarily the individual funds. Second, Morningstar publishes a newsletter called *The Fund Investor* both in monthly hard-copy format and online at www.morningstar.com. Its asset class groupings differ from the AAII, and the same is true for Morningstar's other helpful publication, *The ETF Investor.* Try finding it at your local library, or investigate the free online features. Additionally, don't forget to check whether your brokerage house offers access to Morningstar as a complimentary account benefit. If it does, this is a feature I strongly encourage you to take advantage of. As you dive deeper into your portfolio construction, Morningstar offers a host of tools and resources that add tremendous value to your asset allocation efforts.

Another one of my preferred resources available to aid investors in their asset allocation decisions is StockCharts.com's Interactive PerfCharts. The Perf-Charts tool allows you to quickly plot up to 10 symbols, all overlaid together on the same chart. This provides an easy way to compare performance between multiple assets, be they ETFs, index funds, mutual funds, or individual equities. Using the animation bar at the bottom of the chart, you can adjust the time period you wish to view and dynamically evaluate which symbols have outperformed or underperformed. This visual analysis tool provides a simple, yet highly effective method for narrowing your options down to a select few.

Once I have done this, I dig a bit deeper into the ETFs and mutual funds that appear most promising. Both ETF.com and Morningstar provide detailed individual ETF reports that pack an astonishing amount of information into a concise, accessible format. For mutual funds, I use either Morningstar.com or my broker's comparative tools. Charles Schwab, for example, provides my favorite tool: Compare Funds. This resource allows five symbols to be observed side by side along with an extensive list of additional criteria. Most other brokerages offer similar resources to help guide your mutual fund or ETF decisions. The selection criteria will vary from investor to investor according to personal preferences and individual objectives, but I recommend that a premium be placed on the following elements:

- Relative historical performance
- Expenses
- Portfolio composition
- Assets under management (AUM)
- Alpha, beta, and $R2$
- Management personnel

Correlation Coefficients

The other part of the diversification puzzle you must consider is the correlation coefficients between the asset classes in your portfolio. Correlation is a statistical measure that represents the degree to which the prices of two different securities move relative to each other. Correlation coefficients are expressed within the range of +1.0 to −1.0. If the prices of two securities historically move in the same direction, they will have a positive correlation value that falls somewhere between zero and +1.0. If the two securities historically move in opposite directions, they will have a negative correlation value that falls somewhere between zero and −1.0 (Figure 1.5).

I personally create a 10-year correlation matrix in which I calculate all the correlation values between every possible pair of the 20 asset baskets

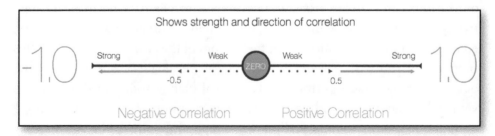

FIGURE 1.5 Correlation Coefficients

in my allocation profile. This helps me visualize and more accurately assess the true diversification level of my portfolio. To expand upon this concept, let me offer this brief example. Assume, for the sake of simplicity, that your asset allocation profile consists of only four asset groups. If you construct a simple four-by-four matrix using your four asset groups, you can then use a simple stock correlation calculator to fill in the matrix. Typically, I calculate the historical relationships between asset groups across the last 10 years. This provides a long-term view that is still relevant to today's market climate. To best solidify this concept, consider a small portfolio that invests in four asset classes, using ETFs for each. After calculating the correlation values between these ETFs, we can compile the data into a four-by-four matrix, which allows us to more accurately understand the portfolio's true level of diversification. Note that while this four-asset profile is small, the foundation and matrix style is the same for a larger portfolio with more asset groups.

To help you quickly calculate statistical correlation values between different assets, there are a number of easy-to-use tools available online. They can be found by running a simple Web search for a stock correlation calculator. The sites returned in this search will allow you to enter two symbols—whether stocks, ETFs, or mutual funds—set the price series interval to either daily, weekly, or monthly, and then select the time period across which you would like their correlation value calculated.

As you construct your asset allocation profile, these correlation values should play a significant role in determining the asset groups you choose and the specific vehicles you use to invest in them. I calculate the correlations among all 20 of the asset groups in my portfolio because of my primary diversification objective. Let us say you invest in 10 different asset groups with correlation values averaging +0.99. While you may feel that your portfolio is diversified because your money is spread across 10 separate asset classes, the correlation values prove that this is only a false sense of security. In reality, your portfolio is not actually diversified. It is not enough to simply choose a collection of asset classes and assume that your portfolio is properly diversified; you must dig deeper to determine the true historical correlations between the asset groups in your portfolio. Diversifying your investments across different assets with low correlation values to each other allows you to design a more efficient portfolio with considerably reduced exposure to downside risk. By utilizing this approach and understanding the specific historical correlation values between the specific asset groups in your portfolio, you can build an asset allocation profile that is better equipped to weather all storms and churn out consistent profits in the long run. If you feel overwhelmed, don't feel ashamed to ask for professional help, particularly if you are new to the investing game. This can be complex stuff!

Let me offer another simple example that illustrates the impact correlation values can have on your portfolio. Suppose that two siblings, Bill and Mary, both inherit equal small fortunes from their parents. They both decide to invest their entire inheritance across four asset baskets. Bill invests his inheritance as follows:

- 25 percent in the S&P 500 (SPY)

- 25 percent in the Industrials Sector (XLI)

- 25 percent in the Consumer Discretionary Sector (XLY)

- 25 percent in the Technology Sector (XLK)

Mary invests her inheritance, equal in value to Bill's, in a different assortment of assets:

- 25 percent in the S&P 500 (SPY)

- 25 percent in the Health Care Sector (XLV)

- 25 percent in the Energy Sector (XLE)

- 25 percent in the Utilities Sector (XLU)

Bill believes he has made some prudent and responsible investment decisions with his inheritance, but in fact the 10-year historical correlation for his portfolio works out to be an average of +0.92. This means his entire portfolio nearly mimics the performance of the S&P 500. This is akin to owning four identical cars in four different colors. Despite his good intentions, Bill did not achieve the diversification and risk reduction he expected. Mary's portfolio, on the other hand, has a much lower historical correlation average, +0.67. By diversifying her investments across a similar collection of assets but with lower historical correlation values, Mary has dramatically reduced the risk exposure of her portfolio and set herself up for a profitable future. Even though Bill had the right idea in spreading his money across an assortment of different asset groups, his failure to consider the correlation values between them weakens his probability of success.

To frame this lesson in one final context, imagine the following: As a longtime Amazon employee, a substantial portion of your compensation package has come in the form of stock options. These options represent a significant share of your total net worth and, intuitively, must be accounted for as you construct a larger investment portfolio. Given the value of these stock options, your financial success is largely dependent on the price performance of Amazon stock, leaving you overly exposed to not only one specific sector within the market but also to one single equity. As such, a primary goal of your portfolio construction efforts should be to offset the risk to which your Amazon options expose you. By finding and investing in other asset groups with low historical correlation values to Amazon specifically—as well as to the consumer discretionary sector, of which Amazon is a part, more broadly—you actively reduce your portfolio's total risk exposure and markedly increase your likelihood of long-term success. The wider you cast your diversification net and the more consideration you give to your portfolio's correlation values, the stronger your probability of success becomes. See Figure 1.6 for an example.

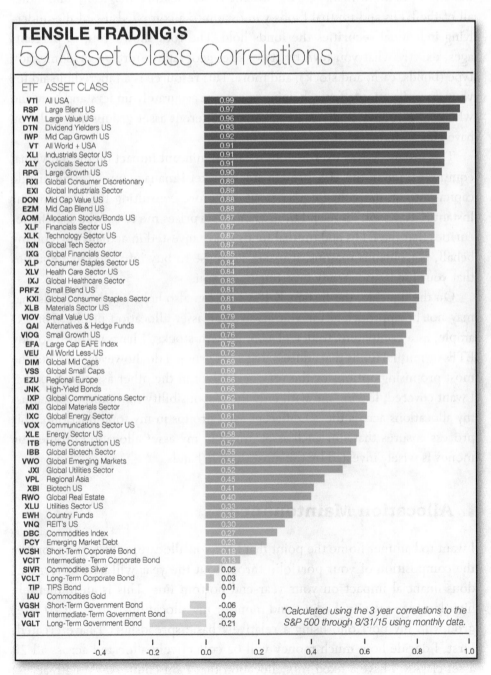

TENSILE TRADING'S
59 Asset Class Correlations

ETF	ASSET CLASS	
VTI	All USA	0.99
RSP	Large Blend US	0.97
VYM	Large Value US	0.96
DTN	Dividend Yielders US	0.93
IWP	Mid Cap Growth US	0.92
VT	All World + USA	0.91
XLI	Industrials Sector US	0.91
XLY	Cyclicals Sector US	0.91
RPG	Large Growth US	0.90
RXI	Global Consumer Discretionary	0.89
EXI	Global Industrials Sector	0.89
DON	Mid Cap Value US	0.88
EZM	Mid Cap Blend US	0.88
AOM	Allocation Stocks/Bonds US	0.87
XLF	Financials Sector US	0.87
XLK	Technology Sector US	0.87
IXN	Global Tech Sector	0.87
IXG	Global Financials Sector	0.85
XLP	Consumer Staples Sector US	0.84
XLV	Health Care Sector US	0.84
IXJ	Global Healthcare Sector	0.83
PRFZ	Small Blend US	0.81
KXI	Global Consumer Staples Sector	0.81
XLB	Materials Sector US	0.8
VIOV	Small Value US	0.79
QAI	Alternatives & Hedge Funds	0.78
VIOG	Small Growth US	0.76
EFA	Large Cap EAFE Index	0.75
VEU	All World Less-US	0.72
DIM	Global Mid Caps	0.69
VSS	Global Small Caps	0.69
EZU	Regional Europe	0.66
JNK	High-Yield Bonds	0.66
IXP	Global Communications Sector	0.62
MXI	Global Materials Sector	0.61
IXC	Global Energy Sector	0.61
VOX	Communications Sector US	0.60
XLE	Energy Sector US	0.58
ITB	Home Construction US	0.57
IBB	Global Biotech Sector	0.55
VWO	Global Emerging Markets	0.55
JXI	Global Utilities Sector	0.52
VPL	Regional Asia	0.45
XBI	Biotech US	0.41
RWO	Global Real Estate	0.40
XLU	Utilities Sector US	0.33
EWH	Country Funds	0.33
VNQ	REIT's US	0.30
DBC	Commodities Index	0.27
PCY	Emerging Market Debt	0.23
VCSH	Short-Term Corporate Bond	0.19
VCIT	Intermediate -Term Corporate Bond	0.13
SIVR	Commodities Silver	0.05
VCLT	Long-Term Corporate Bond	0.03
TIP	TIPS Bond	0.01
IAU	Commodities Gold	0
VGSH	Short-Term Government Bond	-0.06
VGIT	Intermediate-Term Government Bond	-0.09
VGLT	Long-Term Government Bond	-0.21

*Calculated using the 3 year correlations to the S&P 500 through 8/31/15 using monthly data.

-0.4   -0.2   0.0   0.2   0.4   0.6   0.8   1.0

FIGURE 1.6   Tensile Trading's Asset Correlation Coefficients

X-Ray Magic

For the domestic growth stock basket I actively manage, I know exactly what I own, no questions asked. For the other 19 baskets, however, which are managed using ETFs or mutual funds, figuring out exactly what I own is not always as clear. To resolve this issue, Morningstar.com provides another amazingly useful service: the Instant X-Ray tool. After entering all your positions into the site's portfolio manager, the Instant X-Ray feature magically unbundles all of the ETFs and mutual funds you own into a compiled list of the underlying individual securities the funds hold. The tool shows you, in percentages, exactly what you own by style, size, geography (foreign or domestic), type (bonds, cash, and stock), and more. This resource is an incredible aid for your diversification efforts, helping you more accurately understand how and where your money is allocated across the different asset groups in which you have chosen to invest.

This Instant X-Ray exercise often has a significant impact on the individual equities I trade in the U.S. growth stock basket I manage myself. I never pile capital into an individual equity position before consulting the Morningstar Instant X-Ray tool. Time and time again, it surprises me to see the specific securities that the ETFs and mutual funds I have invested in actually own on my behalf. For obvious reasons, it makes no sense to buy into the same equities that your funds are already investing in for you.

On the flip side, the Instant X-Ray tool can also help weed out funds that may not be appropriate for you given your asset allocation profile. For example, as a competent trader of U.S. growth stocks, I have no need to buy ETFs or mutual funds that address that asset group. I do, however, seek out the most promising options or the very best talent in the other asset baskets that I want covered, leaving me with only the responsibility to monitor and adjust my allocations across the 20 different asset groups in my total portfolio. This process ensures that, for each asset group in my asset allocation profile, my money is wisely invested by the most capable hands.

Allocation Maintenance

I want to hammer home the point that how you allocate, adjust, and monitor the composition of your portfolio throughout the year will have a tremendous financial impact on your year-end bottom line. This is an immensely high-leverage activity. I adjust and monitor my allocations across all 20 asset groups in my portfolio using a relatively basic spreadsheet I have created. First, I decide how much money will be collectively allocated across all 20 asset classes. I have a fixed-mix allocation that I am comfortable with across each of the 20 baskets. For example, for the international small-cap basket, I use an allocation of 5 percent of my portfolio. In other words, in a fixed-mix market, I would maintain 5 percent of my total capital in international small-cap equities. In reality, however, I flex allocations around that number based on the present market's expressed favor or disfavor for that particular asset basket. My target allocation for any asset basket will be either above or below that fixed-mix target based on what the market is telling me at that moment. My job then becomes one of merely flowing money into and out of the 20 asset baskets using the best-performing ETFs or mutual funds for each asset group.

I rebalance my portfolio allocations largely based on my in-the-moment observations and gut intuition, but this task can be completed monthly, quarterly, or annually depending on your investment timeline. In addition, modern seasonality tools allow you to track the past performance of your assets averaged over multiple years to determine historical trends that exist throughout the year. You can then use this information to rebalance into or out of different asset classes at their historically likely annual lows or highs. We will discuss seasonality more thoroughly later on, but keep this unique tool in mind.

Each year, there are four checklist items you should complete in order to keep your portfolio properly balanced and poised to succeed in the future.

First, revisit your target allocation mix for your portfolio. Sit down with your financial adviser or your significant other and consider whether there have been any changes to your financial situation, your investment needs, or your personal risk tolerance. If so, adjust your allocation weights accordingly.

Second, review each of the individual asset groups in your allocation profile. Are the asset classes you own still appropriate for your investor self? If you are dissatisfied with the performance of a particular asset group, note that you do not necessarily have to kick it to the curb entirely. Instead, try changing the investment vehicle you are using for that particular basket, switching, for example, from a mutual fund to an ETF or vice versa.

Third, recalculate the correlations among the asset groups in your portfolio. Don't assume that correlation values remain static over time. If you fail to maintain an accurate understanding of the relationships between your asset groups, your diversification and risk minimization objectives will suffer.

Finally, look back at your target allocation weights for each asset class, and rebalance your investments as needed to return to those levels. Understand that this task is best completed over a longer period of time rather than all at once. Do your best to buy into asset groups at their seasonal lows and sell out at seasonal highs. Likewise, endeavor to hit your target allocation weights for each asset group by investing new money gradually over the course of the year, not all at once.

Together, these four allocation maintenance routines will keep your portfolio running smoothly and in line with your core investment objectives throughout the year.

Key Takeaways

At this juncture I should reassure you that it is perfectly natural to feel overwhelmed. Don't worry. I have put you in front of a fire hydrant and invited you to take a drink. Continue on to Stage 2 with the intention of revisiting this first stage again at a later point in time. I suspect that, after working through the material we will cover in the later stages, a second read-through of the Stage 1 content will yield many more valuable insights. This stage has been jam-packed full of information, much of which will make far more sense once we have finished laying the foundation and begun constructing the walls. Rome was not built in a day, and your transformation into a successful investor certainly will not be, either! For now, focus on learning the market's unique vocabulary, begin to write down your personal trading plan, and start to develop an organizational framework for your investing. Above all, enjoy the journey, and have faith in the process.

Your Personal Money Management Outline

1. Personal Trading Philosophy
   - Personal goals and motivations
   - Investing goals and motivations
   - Can I explain my investing philosophy in 60 seconds?
   - What type of investor am I?
   - My personal investing time frame
   - What markets will I trade?
   - My beliefs about money
   - Personal weekly time commitment
   - My strengths and weaknesses
   - What is my trading edge?
2. Money Management
   - Net worth statement
   - Asset protection strategy
   - Estate plan
   - Asset allocation profile and correlation targets
   - Core-and-Explore split
   - Personal money management rules
   - What do I not buy?
   - Rebalancing and seasonality methodology
3. Investor Self
   - Investor self survey
   - Personal roadblocks
   - Keeping a trading journal
   - Personal discipline
   - Stress management techniques
   - Past blunders and blind spots
   - Lessons learned
   - Rating yourself
4. Investing Tools
   - Preferred brokerage houses
   - Organization paradigm
   - Computer hardware
   - Portfolio management software

- Investment accounting software
- Trading program
- Third-party support

5. Trading Methodology

- Idea sources and resources
- Screening methodology
- Key fundamental indicators
- Technical indicators and toolkit
- ChartList organization and layouts
- Watch lists and stalking strategy
- Explicit trading methodology
- Trading rules
- Routines: daily, weekly, monthly, and annually
- Travel routines

6. Risk Management

- Monitoring routines
- Reward-to-risk calculations
- Ladder-in/Ladder-out percentages
- Setting and adjusting stops
- Triggers and alerts
- Asset protection rules
- Profit protection rules

The Business of Investing

In Stage 1, I urged you to find ways to make your investing fun and interesting in order to remain engaged, focused, and motivated. Thinking about your investing as a hobby is useful as you begin to dive into managing your assets, but at the same time, I challenge you to also embrace the mentality of a professional by treating your investing like a real business. This means establishing a trading place, setting routines, and enlisting professional support when you need it. Figure 2.1 illustrates the things you need to consider when approaching investing as a business.

29

■ Ten Invaluable Investing Lessons

From countless charts, trades, and personal battles with the market, I have come away with 10 invaluable lessons that have made me a better, more successful investor. Collectively, they have taught me the immense value of maintaining a disciplined, businesslike mind-set in all aspects related to my investing. Most accomplished investors have learned these very same lessons and hold them in as equally high regard as I do. Think of them as additional probability points that will help increase your likelihood of consistently profitable trading. We have scraped our knees on the turf of the investing field, but if you take these lessons to heart, you will not need to scrape yours as well.

Lesson 1: Build Your Own Trading Place

I have an office in downtown Seattle, approximately 20 minutes from my home. It is a separate space away from the distractions of a household—the TV, the garage, the dog, my family. When I walk through the door of my office,

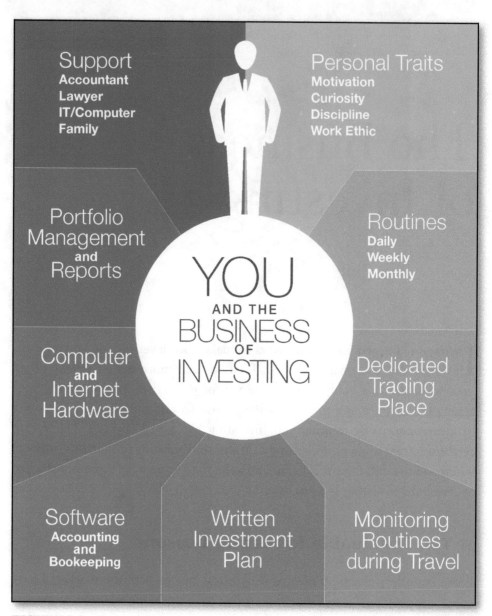

FIGURE 2.1 Business of Investing

fire up my computers, and take a seat at my desk, I am in the game. I put on my investing cap and adopt an entirely different persona. My office sets me in the appropriate market-oriented frame of mind, allowing me to channel the concentration and motivation necessary to trade successfully.

Now, I am a full-time investor, and I understand that leaving home and renting an office is not a feasible option for the majority of you. This is my method, and while it works very well for me, I am by no means suggesting that it is the only way to become a successful investor. I am, however, encouraging you to create your own personal investment place, somewhere that allows you to step away from your other routines, put on your own investing cap, and place yourself in the trader's mind-set. Whether this is in the basement, attic, or garage or at another location entirely—such as a dedicated office—setting up an investment space that gears you up both physically and mentally to trade the stock market is a crucial element in the business of your investing.

Lesson 2: Don't Skimp on the Tools of the Trade

Today's stock market is the essence of a digital world running on Internet time. Gone are the days when you would call your broker to discuss and execute an order for 50 shares of Boeing. The computer has become your broker, and all your trades are now executed online. Having the fastest and most reliable computer setup and network connection is the modern-day equivalent of having the best broker on the trading floor. Although it may seem expensive, buying the latest and greatest computer system on the market is an investment that will pay strong dividends down the road.

Still, your computer is only one piece of the puzzle. Connect it to an external hard drive that automatically backs up your data on a regular basis, and install antivirus and security software to keep your computer bug-free and running safely. Befriend a reliable computer technician who can advise you regarding the ideal setup for your needs, act as your service guru when needed, and effectively diagnose any issues should they arise. Furthermore, the stock market will not close shop when you head out on vacation, so invest in a laptop as well. This way, you can bring your portfolio with you when you are on the go and prevent yourself from falling behind or out of sync in your trading. Investors are nothing without their tools, and a fast, reliable computer system is the single most valuable tool you can have in your arsenal.

Lesson 3: Organization Breeds Profits

Organization, in all its varied forms, is the cornerstone of a prosperous investment plan. From your workspace to your accounting system to your portfolio routines, staying organized is the simplest way to put yourself on the right path and nudge the probabilities in your favor. Physical organization facilitates mental organization and clarity of thought—all of which add up to more money in your pocket at the end of the day. Make a personal pledge to get organized and remain organized, staying on top of your routines, paperwork, passwords, and personal finances. It has been my observation that disorganization induces stress, and stress will directly hinder your investing efforts.

Lesson 4: Harness the Power of a Curious Mind

While they may occasionally make for annoying dinner party guests, info maniacs really do make more money as investors. Developing an intense curiosity about financial and economic movements across the globe, technological developments, demographic changes, politics, and more will help you remain more engaged as an investor. An informed combination of curiosity, education, and determination will support your growth and allow you to consistently realize the profitable opportunities that the market is waiting for you to discover.

I have found that a great way to enhance my curiosity is to occasionally attend investment seminars and conferences. When I return home after spending a day surrounded by other eager investors who are hungry to learn and feed off of one another's energy, I feel thoroughly recharged. One important distinction regarding my attendance, however, is that I am generally uninterested in the speakers' market forecasts and current trading propositions. Instead, I am interested in their systems and methods of analysis. Listening to other experienced investors discuss the tools and routines they employ not only yields new ideas but also spurs powerful self-reflection about my own strategies and techniques. Most investment seminars and conferences can offer something appropriate for every level of investor, from novice to seasoned veteran. After all, self-improvement is an endless journey, and even the world's greatest traders will admit that they still have room to grow. You may have to actively dig for it, but that one gem of trading knowledge that can catapult you to the next level is hiding there somewhere.

Lesson 5: Don't Try to Go It Alone

Don't make the mistake of thinking that your investing is a solo performance. The parents out there will agree: It takes a village to raise a child. As an investor, you need soft support from your friends and family and hard support from your bookkeeper, tax accountant, estate attorney, and information technology (IT) expert. Surrounding yourself with such a team is simply smart business when it comes to your investing. Unfortunately, many investors spend years fighting this reality—to the detriment of their trading. They believe denial is merely a town somewhere in Australia. You must be frank and straightforward in determining what you can do yourself and which areas or tasks would be better managed or accomplished by calling in professional assistance. If you will be more effective by asking your spouse to be your bookkeeper or hiring an accountant to help minimize your taxes, then don't hesitate to make those decisions. Whether you are a full-time trader or a recreational investor, the probability of your success will increase significantly if you are able to involve your family, your significant others, and any professional assistance you need. Help these individuals understand your goals, and they in turn will help you achieve them. Recognize that there are high- and low-leverage activities. By keeping your attention centered on the high-leverage items and delegating responsibility for the low-leverage items to others, you will keep your eyes on the primary objective: maintaining your discipline and focus.

Lesson 6: Keep Up with Legal and Tax Issues

Ongoing changes in our legal structure and tax code can have a dramatic impact on the nature of your investing efforts and your profits. An inexpensive yet effective way to stay current with these changes is to read the American Association of Individual Investors' (AAII) summary of tax changes, published annually. This resource guide provides a straightforward explanation of otherwise complicated and exceedingly lengthy tax codes, and it is essential for minimizing your tax payments and keeping more in your pocket to invest. As your investing becomes more serious and you continue to assume the businesslike mind-set of a professional investor, I recommend you read up on the current advantages and disadvantages—from a tax standpoint—of classifying yourself as a trader versus an investor in the eyes of the Internal Revenue Service (IRS). There are dozens of books and online resources that can offer insightful advice, and I suggest reading a few to familiarize yourself with the topic before you rush in to see your tax attorney or your accountant. That way, when you do meet with these professionals, you will have a firm understanding of your options and be better equipped to make the best and most appropriate decision for your personal situation. In addition, your understanding of your own position will help them help you when it comes time to make these constructive decisions.

Lesson 7: Use Reliable Accounting and Investment Software

Branching off from the get organized pitch, using the proper accounting and portfolio management software is not a luxury—it is a necessity. If you fail to keep accurate and up-to-date records, I can tell you with certainty that you will end up paying more than you owe in taxes and will unnecessarily diminish the profits you have worked so hard to earn. Using second-class investment software will lead you to make second-class investment decisions, and your trading potential will be stifled as a result.

The AAII regularly publishes reviews and ratings of the most widely used and popular software on the market for managing your personal finances and portfolio accounts. I strongly encourage you to invest in the package with the largest market share for the computer platform that you use. This will diminish the likelihood of your software being pulled off the shelves by your vendor, which can be a disaster if you've entered years of data into the program. Don't forget to check the compatibility of these software programs with your brokerage. You want to make sure the latest market pricing data downloads seamlessly and updates all your current positions automatically.

The learning curve for these products is not insignificant, so finding software with a strong market share such that it will likely remain popular is a wise decision. The same can be said of using cloud-based portfolio management programs. Finding an online option with a large, dedicated user base and proven security features for your personal data should be your primary concern. There is an abundance of resources, online and in print, dedicated to helping you find the best accounting and investment software for your particular needs. Take the time to do your homework, choose an appropriate option, and implement it into your management plan.

Lesson 8: Foster an Entrepreneurial Tenacity and Work Ethic

I am a four-time entrepreneur with a background out of Silicon Valley, and many of my closest trading friends are former entrepreneurs themselves. Maybe I am a bit biased, but I believe the entrepreneurial spirit provides an ideal character for managing money. It is important to understand and appreciate that when you trade the stock market and manage your own financial portfolio, you are your own boss. This does not simply mean you are free to do as you like whenever you like, although that may be partly true; rather, take it to mean you are responsible for your own self-management. There is no one else looking over your shoulder, correcting your mistakes, or keeping you in line when you start to drift off course. As such, you must bring to the table an entrepreneurial spirit and a highly motivated work ethic.

As an investor, you can choose what, when, how, and whether to trade. When you approach your investing with energy, confidence, and discipline, committing yourself to work as hard as your time allows, the market can be very generous. Slack off, however, and the investing game can quickly turn into a bloodbath. If you constantly remind yourself that you are the boss and that you are in control—and accept your responsibility to devote yourself wholeheartedly to your investing—you will be rewarded.

The impact of teaching on my own investing has been fascinating. Even after decades of trading, I am strikingly rejuvenated by the company of my students, as if their curiosity and interest were somehow transferred to me. When you surround yourself with others who share a similar passion, their energy seems to rub off in a good way. Whether through educational courses, investment clubs, friends, or family members, I encourage you to seek out these positive relationships and the benefits their interactions can offer.

Lesson 9: Keep Estate Planning in Mind

It takes a good deal of business acumen to accumulate, protect, and grow your wealth. There is a fourth stage to this process, however: passing on your wealth to your loved ones while minimizing Uncle Sam's cut. Proper estate planning is not only something you must do for your beneficiaries' sake, but rather it is also an opportunity for you to truly understand, organize, and plan your finances from start to finish. By staying current on the ever-changing rules and regulations surrounding estate planning, you can ensure your successes in the market live on to see another day in the manner in which you desire. A thorough review of your estate planning can also benefit you in the present by serving as an incentive to stay healthy, exercise, and guarantee that your retirement funds will support you as you live a long, prosperous life. Even so, be sure to meet with your estate-planning attorney every two years in order to keep your plans and paperwork current, regardless of your age or physical state. Trust me, steps like these are not just weightless suggestions; they are good business.

Lesson 10: Put It in Writing!

We have covered this before, but it is a point I cannot emphasize enough: In all settings—from well-managed businesses to professional money managers—documentation is the centerpiece of effective organization and operation. Your task as an individual investor is to adopt the strategies of a business and act like a professional in your approach to the market. To accomplish this task, you must document and update your tools, methodology, and intentions in written form. Professional money managers know and understand from experience that the financial data they must process is too much to keep in their heads. Don't fool yourself into thinking you are unique. The simple exercise of putting pen to paper and writing everything out in front of you will yield valuable insights. I have found this to be the most effective and efficient method of staying properly organized, focused, and on target to accomplish my financial goals.

While it is perhaps true that none of these individual lessons standing alone will radically change your trading experience, it is the control and discipline they provide when bundled together and embraced that will turn the probabilities in your favor. Adopting these behaviors now as you start your journey into the stock market will unlock the successful investor within you and be reflected in your trading profits at the end of the year.

▪ Staying Committed on the Road

I frequently have students ask me how I manage to maintain my investing routines while on the road. Most assume I power down my portfolio and step away from the markets while I am traveling. When I tell them the truth, they are shocked to learn that I actually do the exact opposite, often ramping up my investing when I am away from home or the office. On a springtime trip to Hawaii some years ago, I took a moment to reflect on my investing history and realized, to my surprise, that a disproportionate number of my winning trades had been made while I was on vacation. My trading journals are full of notes written during several dozen trips to Hawaii over a few decades, and the insights are quite striking. The distractions of my daily life back home are minimized on these trips, which allows me to maximize my concentration and find the clarity I need to trade successfully. It is as if the warm island breeze and the peaceful calm of the ocean waves send my senses into overdrive and move me to truly listen to the market. Thousands of miles from the hustle and bustle of Wall Street, I absorb the news and analyze my charts with a healthy, powerful detachment.

The point is this: ignoring your portfolio while you are away from home is simply not an option. Laptops, tablets, and smartphones make it possible to remain perfectly connected wherever you go. Embrace technology when you travel, and use it to continue participating in the markets. I have also found that by making the markets a part of my vacations, I develop positive associations with my investing. I am passionate about my trading, and when I am relaxing by the pool with my laptop in front of me and a cocktail in my hand, that passion is only rejuvenated. Wall Street will not wait for you to catch a flight back to reality, so it is your responsibility to maintain your routines and stay focused on your investing no matter where you are. All it takes is a little discipline and devotion.

▪ The Investor's Quad

Before we move on to Stage 3, I would like to introduce a concept I call the Investor's Quad. For many of my students and me, this has been a valuable long-term metaphor to stabilize us throughout our investing journeys. Imagine a baseball field with its four bases. To reach first base, you will need education and information. We are nothing without knowledge, so the first step must be to immerse ourselves in learning. As we discussed earlier in this stage, you can realize the profits that the market is waiting for you to discover by developing an intense curiosity and educating yourself about the stock market, the global economy, and current world events. Information facilitates growth as an investor, and your curiosity will become the compass that guides you.

Making it to second base requires tools and organization. There are an endless number of resources available to you, all offering a limitless array of tools that promise to make you more money. Many popular charting programs alone offer more than 300 technical indicators from which to choose. Narrow these down to a manageable collection that aligns with your goals and objectives, then focus your energy on maximizing your results with these. From your desk to your computer system to your written money management plan, stay organized both physically and emotionally so you can be as efficient and productive as possible. An effective organization system at the most basic level will translate to similar organization at every next step along the way, all the way up to your portfolio itself, and will increase your probability of consistently profitable trading.

Third base requires analysis and routines. As you continue to develop the foundation for your investing and transition your focus toward asset growth, the routines and analysis procedures you establish will become the lifeblood of your investing. A diligent commitment to the effective routines and analysis methods you adopt in your money management plan will position you for success and wave you around third.

The first three bases count for very little if you do not bring it home and score. To make it there, though, you must free your investor self to take action and execute your trading. We will learn more about the investor self in Stage 3. As we move through the remaining stages of stock market mastery, we will return frequently to the bases of the Investor's Quad, delving deeper into the meaning and importance of each to provide greater direction as you continue to develop your complete investment system.

Key Takeaways

- Stage 2 is all about how to treat your investing like a business, whether you are just starting out in the markets or have been trading for years. There are 10 lessons that every trader must embrace before finding success. They are:
  1. Build your own trading place.
  2. Don't skimp on the tools of the trade.
  3. Accept that organization breeds profits.
  4. Harness the power of a curious mind.
  5. Don't try to go it alone. Your support network matters.
  6. Keep up with legal and tax issues. Don't be afraid to seek professional help when necessary.
  7. Use reliable accounting and investment software.
  8. Foster an entrepreneurial tenacity and work ethic.
  9. Keep estate planning in mind.
  10. Put it in writing!
- Every investor's style, system, and goals are different, but the common thread among successful investors is that they approach their trading with a sense of professionalism.

(continued)

Key Takeaways (*Continued*)

- While developing your system and routines, bear in mind that they should be flexible and portable. A change of location—be it on vacation or while traveling for work—is no excuse to ignore your portfolio and take a break from the markets. Modern technology allows you to take your investing with you on the road, so take advantage of tools that give you the ability to trade wherever you are.
- Finally, remember the Investor's Quad. Education and information will get you to first base; tools and organization will bring you to second. Analysis and routines are required to make it to third. After that, only freeing your investor self can help you bring it home.

The Investor Self

The average investor would be utterly perplexed at witnessing the effortless manner in which money often flows into the accounts of exceptional, experienced traders. Contrary to popular belief, these consistently profitable investors are no different from the rest of us. What makes them successful is that they have developed intense discipline, concentration, and emotional controls that allow them to stay firmly focused on their goals and remain grounded at all times. The integration of cognitive psychology with the world of investing has spawned the field of modern behavioral finance. To our great benefit, this field has allowed us to learn and better understand—with tremendous specificity—exactly what the ideal investor looks like. In addition, it has proven that it is in fact possible for the average investor to model and adopt winning behaviors and psychological attributes. Incorporating these characteristics into your own trading style will enhance your investment record and fuel your personal growth in the process. Regardless of your level of experience, emotions play a major role in your investing. With the correct guidance, mental conditioning, and practice, however, you can develop the very same habits and emotional controls that feed the success of professional investors and money managers. To do so, you must be willing to cultivate and shape your investor self.

I have always maintained that the secret to success in the stock market is composed of two basic pieces. The first obviously involves the strategic, technical aspects of investing—the numbers, charts, and methodologies. The other 50 percent, however, is the investor self. Learning how to achieve and maintain a functional equilibrium in this arena is crucial. Trading the stock market is a tough and emotionally charged endeavor. Research has proven beyond a shadow of a doubt that investors perform better when they acknowledge this and when they can anticipate how their emotions will affect their trading behavior. As such, nurturing both halves of this equation is vital for profitable and consistent investing.

■ The Five Levels of Investor Growth

As you jump into the stock market and begin your investing journey, you must pass through five levels of investor growth (Figure 3.1). These levels are not an option, and despite how eager and ready you may be, you cannot skip from the first level to the fifth and become an expert investor overnight. As a novice at level one, your priority is to not lose money and simultaneously gain foundational experience. Education is your sidekick as you develop an ever-important curiosity and explore the resources available to you online, in print, and at live investor events. You have a wide assortment of tools at your disposal and should experiment with many different options to find the ones that make the most sense to you, that you feel comfortable with and trust will be effective in helping you accomplish your investment goals. At this level, immerse yourself in reading to absorb as much information and knowledge as possible.

At the second level, you become an advanced beginner; you start to put what you have learned to use and carefully invest in the market. Your goal now is to begin making money—small amounts at a time, but on a regular and consistent basis. Having experimented with a handful of tools, strategies, and other market resources, your handcrafted and personalized tool kit is beginning to take shape. By carefully investing in the market, you are starting to walk the walk.

Once you have developed a record of consistently profitable trades, you are ready to make the transition to the third level: that of a competent investor. Here, your objective is to maximize the personal returns on your investments. The keys to your success now become discipline, focus, and commitment

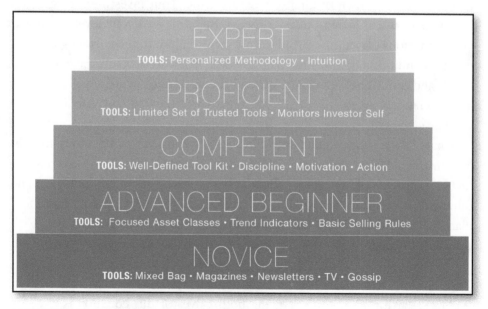

FIGURE 3.1   The Five Levels of Investor Growth

to your goals. Your tool kit is becoming increasingly well defined, and your trading profits are more consistent as a result. Over time, you will begin to develop a heightened sense of the market, thereby promoting you to a proficient investor, level four. Your routines now become second nature, and your intuition will allow you to begin extending yourself to test your abilities and trade based less on simple facts, figures, and guidelines and more on your innate belief system. Your tool kit will be pruned down to a core set that you trust deeply and has proven to be consistently effective and profitable in the past. From here, you make the final leap into the fifth level: an expert investor. Trading is a state of mind centered around your battle-tested intuition and controlled by the rigid self-discipline you have worked hard to develop. Your trading plan has become a well-oiled machine that drives your portfolio to consistently profitable returns.

This road to the expert stage may appear long and daunting, but my goal in outlining this process is to paint for you a realistic picture of what it takes to trade the markets at this higher level. It is my sincere hope that, by doing so, I can help you determine exactly what type of investor you want to become. If you have the drive and determination to fully commit your time and energy— both emotionally and physically—to becoming an expert investor, then I applaud you. If the preceding levels satisfy your goals, fit well with your time constraints, or feel appropriate for the energy you are willing to devote to the market, then the decision to jump off the train at Level 2 or 3 may be the right one for you and is equally worthy of praise. When you trade the markets you know and understand, in a time frame that suits your lifestyle and with the methodology most tailored to your personality, you will find your way and begin to produce consistent profits. It is not about finding the one right way to invest; rather, it is about finding the one right way for *you personally* to invest. In order to make the right decisions given the host of factors that affect your investing, however, you need to put your hopes and dreams aside, focus only on the realities of your situation, and look deep within to evaluate yourself with a sense of utterly brutal, completely candid honesty. By assessing yourself at this depth and determining your strengths and weaknesses as an investor, you will unlock your growth and get in touch with your investor self in a uniquely intimate, exceptionally powerful fashion.

Over many years, I have tracked my own personal transformation into a mature trader. Along the way, I have passed a number of key road markers signaling important developments. As I grew, I moved away from self-criticism and began trending toward honest and constructive self-assessment. Early on, I evaluated my trading experiences simply according to how I felt. Later, however, I transitioned into evaluating my experiences according to the amount of emotional control I exercised during a trade. As a novice investor, I often suffered at the hands of doubt and fear, hindrances that I have overcome and replaced with faith and confidence in myself and my trading system. Finally, in the beginning stages of my investing career, I was an info maniac, vacuuming up anything and everything in sight. Despite all this information, I struggled with the basics, and my returns were stifled as a result. Simplicity, I discovered, is an objective that promotes profitability. As a mature investor, I now have a depth of understanding that allows me to filter out and ignore much of today's wasteful market noise.

My point in describing these personal transformations is to point out that successful investing is about much more than data, charts, and strategies. There is always a gap between what an investor has written out as his or her trading system and the actual working implementation of that system. I call this the "rubber-band gap," that distance between your system and your mastery over yourself. Early on, the relationship between the two stretches out and rockets back with a painful snap. As you establish this mastery over your own behaviors and emotions, the volatility between the two diminishes. Your intuition becomes more highly developed and can be relied upon to deliver desirable results. When mastery of your trading system is paired with a mastery of your investor self, the combination becomes virtually invincible.

Novice investors believe in the gospel of acquisition—"just give me the right tools and let me run wild." Seasoned investors know, however, that the gospel of transformation, not acquisition, is what they will need to truly succeed. These investors have experienced the prerequisite conversion from emotional rags to investment riches. When a novice investor finally reaches this realization, the lights go on and he or she inevitably exclaims, "Oh, now I get it!" It is at this point that the real trading can begin. The adrenaline will always be there—that is, in part, why we trade in the stock market—but the extremes after this realization will be modulated and controlled. I can teach you the methodology and provide you with the foundational tools, but whether you master the stock market will be determined in large part by your ability to transform your investor self and develop the necessary behavioral attributes to become a profitable trader. Carving out some time amid the bustle of a trading day to engage in some introspection about your emotional status will keep you respectful of its importance and encourage your personal improvement as an investor.

■ Investor Weaknesses

The legendary Great Bear of Wall Street, Jesse Livermore, once said, "Know yourself before you trade. The market is an expensive place to learn." Most successful investors will tell you that with hard work and honest self-evaluation, nearly anyone can become a profitable trader. Together, these are the two necessary ingredients required in the recipe for successful investing: one large serving of hard work mixed in with a generous pinch of brutal honesty. When we sit down to reflect and analyze ourselves, it is easy to think about what we do well and come up with a long list of strengths. The challenge is determining our weaknesses with equally truthful consideration.

Throughout several of my classes some years ago, I conducted an anonymous survey of many dozens of investors across a wide spectrum of experience levels, asking them to record anything and everything they suspected was keeping them from becoming the very best investor they believed they could be. Even with respect to my own trading, the results of this enlightening experiment were supremely profound and exceptionally powerful. Upon compiling the responses, it became clear that the struggles these investors shared fell into four distinct categories:

1. Planning roadblocks
2. Deficiencies in knowledge and education
3. Personal psychological baggage and beliefs
4. Execution barriers

As you read these confessions, ask yourself which apply to you, and think about what it will take for you to conquer them.

Planning Roadblocks

- I plan my trades in my head. I struggle to write them down.

- I do not plan for or consider tax consequences or how to minimize them when I trade.

- I love tech stocks. My asset allocation is always off-kilter because I overweight that sector.

- I bounce around with the weekly market winds. I have no niche or investment focus.

- I am not good with rules. I do not really have any trading rules.

- I am not sure what money management is, and I do not think I have any.

- I am disorganized and seem to lack the skills to change for the better.

- I have too many different trading plans. I cannot stay focused on just one.

- I do not have enough time to complete my daily and weekly routines.

- I have an investing plan for buying stocks but not for selling them.

Deficiencies in Knowledge and Education

- I need to know why before I trade, and I waste time searching endlessly for an answer.

- I am an information junkie. I never seem to have enough information.

- I lack information discretion and believe everything I read and hear from the latest guru.

- I am too slow to learn from my past mistakes and often find myself repeating them.

- I lack the energy to focus, so I do not acquire the appropriate expertise.

- I have learned how to use lots of different tools, but they seem to be the wrong ones.

- I have been reluctant to embrace new technology and software, and I feel left behind.

- I am too cynical. I do not believe anyone is willing to help me become a better investor.

Personal Psychological Baggage and Beliefs

- Emotionally, I struggle to cut my losses and get out of a stock when the price is falling.

- I have trouble changing my behavior even when I know I must.

- I continue to procrastinate and miss the opportunities I see in the market.

- My outlook is pessimistic, and my fears overwhelm me. I am too afraid of losing money.

- I am impatient, impulsive, indecisive, and inconsistent. I am too emotional overall.

- I am an adrenaline junkie. I cannot stick to my plan and instead try to go for the quick reward.

- I lack the discipline to execute my methodology consistently.

- I let my personal problems and my immediate emotional state affect my trading.

Execution Barriers

- The price always feels too high or too low, so I do not take action.

- I watch price movements too closely and lose sight of the trend and the big picture.

- My trading frequency is out of balance. I trade too much or I do not trade enough.

- The size of my trades is regularly off, and I often juggle too many positions.

- My timing is poor. I rush to buy and rush to sell, often without proper analysis.

- I suffer from analysis paralysis and fail to pull the trigger despite seeing an entry.

- I fall in love with my positions and become too emotionally attached.

It takes considerable mental control and determination to overcome these personal hurdles, but I assure you that by starting with truly honest self-assessment, you will gain a pure and accurate picture of your investor self. This will become your secret weapon on your path toward mastery of the stock market. Before venturing out in search of your own trading edge, it is vital that you address each of these four common areas of weakness. Take the time now to sit down with a cup of coffee and be open and straightforward with yourself about your weaknesses. Just as with so many other pieces of your investing puzzle, this is a decision that will pay substantial dividends later on. As you delve deeper and deeper into the stock market, your failure to overcome these hurdles could become a very costly decision. For now, consider that the secret to your investing success boils down to the simple elements displayed in Figure 3.2.

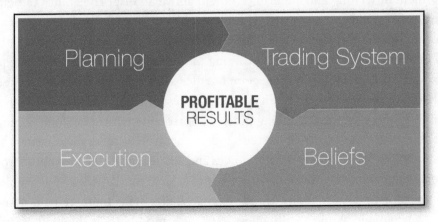

FIGURE 3.2 The Key Elements of Profitable Investing

■ Learn from the Professionals

At an investment conference in San Francisco, I had the pleasure of spending an afternoon talking with a successful European money manager. We spoke at length about the type of people his firm hires as portfolio managers. Among the numerous attributes he discussed, he said that the firm looked for what he referred to as "double-minded" individuals. In essence, the firm wanted someone with the ability to look into their personal mirror and see their daily self reflected back while at the same time, when looking into their market mirror as a professional manager, see the reflection of an entirely different individual—that of an investor with a separate set of emotional attributes more appropriate for trading the market. The ability to look at your own reflection in two distinct mirrors and accept the different realities of the two reflections—never letting one vision pollute the other—is both rare and exceptional. More commonly, traders see their face in the market's mirror but fail to acknowledge the unflattering image staring back at them. Instead, they create a less effective, wishful image of themselves. These traders tend to give in to their need to experience short-term pleasures, often at the cost of long-term profitability.

Understand that exceptional investors possess a collection of attributes and skills that, together, add up to a distinct edge in their trading. Consciously and diligently developed in each individual over time, these attributes have been labeled and identified thanks to modern research into behavioral finance. The market will humble even the wisest and strongest among us and therefore must be approached with great humility. Leave your ego at the door because the market will undoubtedly charge you for it otherwise.

Seasoned investors display a persistent and unquenchable motivation to accomplish their goals and master the art of investing. They have personally developed hands-on strategies that fit their trading personalities, documenting them in writing and adhering to them above all else. The ability to be relentlessly candid and objective with themselves in regards to their beliefs and weaknesses is a primary focus. Their inner resiliency allows them to weather all market storms with minimal scarring to their attitude and emotional equilibrium. Well-defined risk management rules are a centerpiece of their methodologies, along with an ability to accept responsibility for loss with both humility and a forward-thinking outlook. Seasoned investors exhibit an unassailable confidence in their system and in themselves, and they harness the discipline to follow their methodologies and act decisively. They show a strong work ethic, working not only harder but also smarter. Patience and an ability to wait for high-probability trades to materialize help them remain consistently profitable, while a willingness to change, modify their thinking, rewrite their methodologies, or transform themselves as needed keeps them always in tune with their investor selves. Last but not least, they understand the immeasurable value of being willing to accept a subservient role to a higher power: the markets.

Truly successful portfolio managers are the gods of Wall Street and compensated tremendously for their unique skill sets. What you as an individual investor need to take away from this is that it is not, in fact, these investors' superior tools or cutting-edge methodologies that facilitate their extraordinary performance. These days, their tool kits are not so different from those available to us as individual investors. Rather, what sets them apart is their nurtured ability to vaccinate themselves against the destructive human tendencies that naturally surface when most of us attempt to trade the markets. As an aspiring investor, you must convince yourself that you can and will embrace the attributes of these professional money managers, weaving them into the fabric of your own investing to overcome your personal roadblocks, suppress negative tendencies, and become the investor you know you can be.

■ Your Daily Journal

Profitable behavior is based on good organizational routines, flexible thinking, consistent discipline, and self-control. Acknowledging your strengths and weaknesses as you go about outlining and analyzing your investor self is your ticket to success in the stock market, and for that reason, I recommend keeping a daily trading journal.

This is the turbocharged vehicle that will allow you to do so faster and more efficiently. It is a routine I embraced long ago and continue to rely on each day without exception. In describing for you the structure of my personal journal, I encourage you to customize yours and mold it to fit your own unique personality. Given the importance of this routine, it is imperative that you do what it takes to make it a fun, engaging, enjoyable experience rather than a burden or a source of stress. By developing a structure that works for you and making it a product of your creative ingenuity, your journal will become an invaluable resource and a catalyst for your development as an investor. My suggestion is that you approach your journal outline as you would a dinner buffet: Pick and choose the elements that best suit your palate, and leave behind those that do not appeal.

In addition to the journal itself, I carry small, pocket-sized notepads with me at all times. They are conveniently placed in my suit jacket pockets, my gym bag, my carry-on luggage, and all of my family's cars. For years, I have used these notepads to jot down whatever I hear, see, or think of spontaneously. More recently, I have begun using my smartphone in lieu of the pen and paper, because the convenience of an infinite virtual notepad is hard to overlook. Together, these resources have become my primary tool for observational living. Opportunities surround us in abundance if we open ourselves up to them, and I find that small, brilliant little gems present themselves in the most unlikely situations. It is uncanny how often these observations translate into profitable investment decisions somewhere down the line. I am not rigid in what I write down, but I do label most of my notes under four categories:

1. **Lessons:** Enlightening or instructional experiences I have had.
2. **Facts:** Actualities supported by some evidence that a majority would deem true.
3. **Rules:** Personal standards of behavior I embrace and that govern my conduct in a majority of situations.
4. **Principles:** Truths or assumptions I embrace, which then become a personal characteristic and part of my ethical code.

These notepads have become a feeder mechanism for my daily journal, and the mere act of transferral into the journal's pages is a powerful learning process that cements my observations into a more permanent format. My daily journal itself is divided into, again, four sections: personal items, market notes, new ideas, and refinements. Each day, I begin journaling by writing about something unrelated to the market—something memorable and positive to help me step into the right frame of mind. By documenting my physical and emotional state, incorporating everything from my energy level to my confidence to my anxieties, I am able to peer into my inner life and rate myself on a scale from 1 to 10. As I look back at my winning and losing trades to see what lessons I can learn from both, this rating scale becomes an effective way of assessing how my personal state affects my trading.

After gauging my own mood, I focus on the mood of the market. I have my own personal checklist that helps me note my observations. I review yesterday's market close and the current morning's European markets as well. I devise both bullish and bearish scenarios for today's markets and even for tomorrow's, and each day I reflect and comment on yesterday's scenarios. If anything is particularly confusing or random about the markets, I address those items in the market notes section. To close out this section of my journal, I consider what my general reaction will be to the market today, from the viewpoint of either a buyer, a seller, or a stops adjuster. Much of this is done when the market is closed.

From here, I move on to the new ideas section of the journal, which serves as my daily creative brainstorming session, challenging my observational powers and giving me permission to dream big, bold, and outrageously. I often look back to track my best ideas after they have developed into profitable investments, and I find that the majority of them begin here. This section of my journal has taught me to accept change and, in fact, seek it out because change creates opportunity, and the market will reward you for identifying these opportunities before the masses do. My objective here is to visualize the markets from a completely fresh perspective, thinking outside the box and allowing myself to explore the extent of my creativity in the process.

Finally, I turn to the refinement section of my journal. Having explored my personal self, my observations, and my creativity, it is time to flip the switch and become a serious investor, determined to improve my trading results. I carefully study my mistakes and my successes, my winning trades and my losing trades, and reflect on the lessons they offer. It is imperative here that I be brutally honest with myself in examining my previous behaviors. I want to know whether I let any weak emotions sabotage my decision making, whether I followed my system and stayed true to my methodology, or whether I became sentimentally attached to a stock and let a trade become personal. I question my execution and assess any potential areas for improvement. By delving deep into my personal strengths and weaknesses and documenting what I have learned from my investing experiences, the refinement section of my daily trading journal keeps me in touch with my investor self and helps me remain intently focused on the relevant goals, objectives, and priorities of my emotional growth as an investor.

My journal structure is a personal formula that I have developed over many years. Again, I encourage you to work as hard as possible at shaping your journal into a format that fits your investor self. Having said that, there are a few guidelines you should follow to ensure you maintain an effective trading journal.

First and foremost, you must write the journal yourself. This should be a chance for you to be thoroughly honest with yourself in a completely private format, away from any other set of eyes. Fear that others might read your journal can tarnish your ability to be honest, so privacy is of the utmost importance. Your journal is yours and yours alone, and by keeping it that way, you allow yourself to speak openly and truthfully without concern for the opinions of others. If it is worth living or trading, write it down. Your journal should showcase your powers of observation and provide you with an outlet for expressing and documenting anything and everything that you see, think, and feel. Next, the time you devote to your journal should be focused and directed. Shut the door, ignore the phone, close your Internet browser, and turn your eyes away from your e-mail. These interruptions will only detract from the purity and honesty of the critical observations you record in your journal.

Another guideline: Listen to the market and let it educate you. It wants to speak to you, but you must be receptive enough to hear what it has to say. Use your journal to learn from your mistakes and those of other traders you have read about, but express these lessons as positive and constructive statements you can learn from and use to guide you. When your journal begins to look like a scrapbook—with clippings pasted to its pages and various highlighter colors embellishing your comments—then you will know that you have truly arrived. At this point, your journal will have become your confidant, your growth facilitator, and your personal educator. In the stock market, reflecting on the past should be an opportunity for personal growth, not a source of negative memories and emotions. Clarity in detailing the lessons you have learned will benefit you greatly down the road.

As you write your journal, remember to stay true to the system that you have created for yourself in your money management plan. Don't redefine yourself as an investor each day to suit the current market. Have faith in the plan you have laid out for yourself, and stay true to this course. Most important, discipline yourself to make this a daily routine, but again, do what it takes to keep it fun and engaging. (It is okay to miss a day!) Also remember that, as I have said before, I am sharing with you my world as a full-time investor; your world likely differs. After all, it involves a separate career and other demands on your time that may render daily journaling a near impossibility. It is perfectly acceptable for your routines to reflect this reality and for you to visit your journal on a weekly basis rather than a daily basis.

Once you have learned all that you need to know about technical and fundamental analysis and written a sound and effective trading plan, developing and strengthening your mental discipline becomes a high-leverage activity that will undoubtedly have a significant influence on your progress. This is the personal element of trading that distinguishes you from others, the element that explains why no two investors are able to trade the same way. Your mental discipline must be cultivated, tended to, and exercised with proper care and diligence. When you truly appreciate the importance of mental discipline and how it will positively impact your trading, the personal and behavioral rules and routines you establish for yourself will facilitate this discipline and keep you focused.

Keeping a personal journal to record and assess your trading activities is central among these routines. As you develop your journaling style and settle into it, aspire to become an objective observer and a tough-minded decision maker, able to put your ego aside and truthfully trade the market you see in front of you. It is important that you take pride in your ability to maintain a mental and physical equilibrium. The process of recording your observations, analysis, and emotions surrounding the market will foster this ever-important balance. Your aspiration should be to invest in the financial markets with a mind-set that is appropriate for your investor self and can be maintained consistently. It is from this mind-set that your ability to replicate successful trades will emanate, producing profits and steady returns for years to come.

Key Takeaways

- The secret to success in the stock market is understanding the psychology of your investor self and learning to control the common emotional inefficiencies in trading the markets. You must be brutally honest with yourself and know your strengths and weaknesses as you pass through the five levels of investor growth: novice, advanced beginner, competent, proficient, and expert.
- There are four types of weaknesses that investors encounter at all levels: planning roadblocks, knowledge/education deficiencies, psychological baggage, and execution barriers. Each of these errors corresponds to one of the key elements of profitable investing.
- Most important, record your trading experiences in a trading journal. This will make it easier for you to uncover patterns, avoid repeating mistakes, and maintain equilibrium in your investing. If you are candid about your investments, your journal will become a powerful guide to consistent profitability.

Market Analysis

At every hour, every minute, and every second, from Hong Kong to New York, somewhere in the world a financial market is open. Increased globalization and the digital nature of today's financial industry allow you to trade 24 hours a day, to your heart's content. As an investor attempting to figure out what, where, and how to invest in these markets, you are bombarded with a constant and endless stream of information. At times, it can feel as if you are trying to grab a drink of water from a fire hose.

To be a successful investor, you must be able to sift through, process, and interpret this endless information effectively so you can uncover the profitable opportunities the market is offering you. It is for this very reason that the first rule of investing is to narrow your focus to a realistically manageable basket of equities. It is generally not possible to trade commodities and equities continuously across the 12 major global exchanges. Instead, choose an arena you feel genuinely interested in, and build your routines around the realities of that market. A clear, well-designed methodology (and the discipline to follow it) will allow you to assemble your own tool kit of indicators and establish analysis routines and procedures that reflect the realities of your time constraints. This in turn will allow you to efficiently and consistently make profitable investment decisions.

Year in and year out, the results I see and lessons I learn when I flip back through my trading journal lead me to the same simple conclusion: the vast majority of my profitable, winning trades materialize when I diligently follow my methodology. I have hammered this point home already, but I truly cannot stress it enough. Even after more than 25 years as a full-time investor, I still find myself needing a regular reminder to stay focused and true to what I have written in my trading plan. A shocking number of my losing trades reflect a temporary deviation from the trading path I know I should follow. I am human, and these embarrassing breakdowns in discipline happen to all of us. Having said that, understand that you will still experience some losing trades, even when you execute your methodology to a T. A good losing trade occurs when you follow your rules, routines, and methodology, but a bad losing trade occurs when you fail to do so. Losing is a normal part of the probabilities of investing. What will define you as an investor, however, is the lessons you learn from and your response to these losses.

My objective in outlining my personal methodology is to help you visualize a working model and begin to decide for yourself how you will design and develop your own. My methodology is composed of three key elements: permission to buy, telescope-to-microscope approach, and charting indicators.

■ Permission to Buy

This first component in my methodology contains the following six chart-based modules, which allow me to ascertain my most appropriate position in the market, whether it is as a buyer, a holder, or a seller. They are as follows:

1. **Trend of the Market**

   Just as the name implies, this module contains charts of a number of broad-based indexes. The market can only be in one of three modes: an uptrend, sideways movement within a trading range, or a downtrend. Viewing these indexes in different time frames provides an unambiguous answer to the question of which mode the market is currently in.

2. **Allocations**

   This module addresses the questions that must be answered to optimize your asset allocation decisions. The charts clearly show whether large institutions are favoring large-cap, mid-cap, or small-cap stocks. It also shows whether the current market is oriented more toward growth or toward value. The same holds for international versus U.S. markets, U.S. dollars versus bonds, and other key intermarket analyses.

3. **Breadth, Volume, and Volatility**

   This answers key questions pertaining to breadth (the extent of participation by all equities in the present market), volume analysis (whether the money flow is positive or negative), and volatility, sometimes referred to as the fear index. These are all key elements in assessing the current psychology of the market.

4. **Sector Analysis**

   Using charts populated by the eleven Standard & Poor's (S&P)-sector exchange-traded funds (ETFs) and indexes, I address the issue of how the broad sectors of the market presently stack up.

5. **Industries**

   Charts of the industries that comprise each of the S&P sectors allow me to dive down deeper to find the strongest industry in the strongest sector within an uptrending market.

6. Equities

This final module highlights the best-of-the-best individual equities within the strongest industry groups and best sectors.

It should be noted that this system of progressively drilling down deeper into the market—from the highest level of broad indexes all the way to individual equities—is not necessary for all investors. In fact, a very strong argument can be made that individual investors with stricter time constraints, such as a full-time job, can execute a highly profitable strategy of trading only sectors and industries and never buying individual stocks. Finding the investment opportunities most appropriate for your personal constraints is crucial. With today's access to thousands of ETFs and mutual funds covering every global market, this has become a perfectly acceptable option.

■ Telescope-to-Microscope Approach

The second element of my methodology focuses on the power of varied time frames, analyzing the market through a series of lenses, each one smaller and more exact than the previous. I call this the *telescope-to-microscope* approach. The objective of this increasingly defined analysis system is to align the trends of the market at every level, thereby shifting the odds in my favor.

Beginning with a large telescopic lens, I bring the big picture into view, analyzing charts of the market as a whole by looking at 10 years of weekly and monthly data. This allows me to gain a historical understanding of the market and an idea of its general direction. Next, I pull out my spyglass to fine-tune my focus to an intermediate two-year time frame. Then, dialing in the focus once again, I use my magnifying glass to bring the short-term picture into view as I look at daily charts of various indexes over the past six months. Finally, I put my microscopic lens to work, concentrating on charts using 20 days of minute-to-minute data. This allows me to clearly see the current money flow.

I have described the telescope-to-microscope approach as it applies to broad indexes, but I apply the same charting analysis to individual equities as well. The historical insights you can gain regarding potential support and resistance areas when using this strategy are immensely useful, and they can help you stay true to the time frame you have decided is most comfortable for your investing style.

To further empower your investing probabilities, I suggest you combine the telescope-to-microscope approach with a top-down strategy that analyzes potential investments from market to sector to industry to stock (Figure 4.1). Filtering my analysis through these smaller and smaller lenses allows me to find the best stock in the strongest industry in the strongest sector of an uptrending market. There is no denying that the probability of profitable

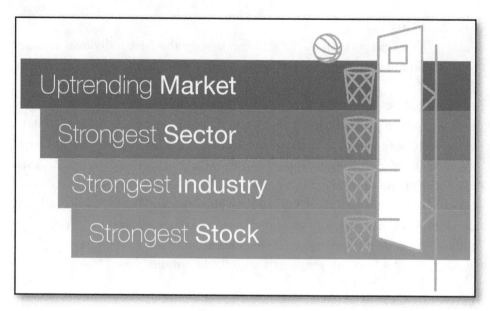

FIGURE 4.1   Sharpshooting with Top-Down Analysis

trading under these conditions is vastly increased. To fall back on a baseball metaphor, I ensure that a trade touches all four bases: At first base, I buy into a position when the market is trending up. At second base, I buy into one of the top two performing sectors. At third base, I buy into one of the top-performing industries in that sector, and at home plate, I buy the strongest stock in that industry group—all while investing in the time frame that best suits my investor self.

The bottom line here is simple. Focusing only on the hot stock selection of the week when buying may make for scintillating conversation at your next cocktail party, but it is unlikely to put real money into your pocket on a recurring basis. Forget the cocktail party temptation and focus instead on a properly structured market-analysis paradigm that will systematically increase your probability of extracting profits from the market. The chart in Figure 4.2 provides a real-world example of a powerful stock pick that has successfully touched all four bases.

■ Charting Indicators

The third and last element of my methodology is my tool kit of charting indicators. Many eager investors have a hard time accepting the concept that less is often more. They become lost in the endless array of indicators, tools, resources, and opinions to which they are exposed. Some available analysis programs offer more than 300 different technical indicators. While many of these may be intellectually stimulating, I am more interested in making profitable trades. Without a dedi-

Inside the image:

AAPL Apple, Inc. Nasdaq GS
24-Nov-2014
— Apple, Inc./Vanguard Total Stock Market ETF 43.13% (24 Nov)

Open 114.89 High 116.78 Low 114.67 Last 116.64 Volume 47.7M Chg +2.12 (+1.85%) ▲
© StockCharts.com

1st base: **Stock vs. Market**

— Technology Select Sector SPDR/Vanguard Total Stock Market ETF 7.46% (24 Nov)

2nd base: **Sector vs. Market**

— Dow Jones US Computer Hardware Index/Technology Select Sector SPDR 21.33% (24 Nov)

3rd base: **Industry vs. Sector**

— Apple, Inc./Dow Jones US Computer Hardware Index 9.78% (24 Nov)

4th base: **Stock vs. Industry**

Apple, Inc. (Daily) 116.64 (24 Nov)
— EMA(20) 109.64
— MA(50) 102.84
— MA(185) 90.88
⬛ Volume 47,691,600

FIGURE 4.2 Covering All Four Bases
Source: Chart courtesy of StockCharts.com.

cated set of core indicators with which you have bonded and grown to intimately understand, your investing will lack direction. Your performance will suffer because you will have deprived yourself of the trust necessary to execute trades based on what the markets and your indicators are telling you. From my own experience and a host of academic studies, the magic number of indicators most investors should use in their analysis is 10. My personal trading tool kit looks at the five essential elements of an equity, then utilizes 10 technical indicators to further determine the present status of each element.

I. Price Action versus the Market
    1. Price Relative
II. Trend Indicators
    1. Trend Lines
    2. Moving Averages
    3. Average Directional Index (ADX)

III. Volume Indicators
　　1. Chaikin Money Flow
　　2. On-Balance Volume
IV. Momentum Indicators
　　1. Relative Strength Index (RSI)
　　2. Moving Average Convergence Divergence (MACD)
　　3. Stochastics
V. Reward-to-Risk Indicators
　　1. Point-and-Figure Charts

Examples of these indicators are illustrated in Figure 4.3.

By diligently using my core set of indicators, I have developed a thorough understanding of each individually, and I instinctively know how and when to best apply them. They have become second nature, and my in-depth knowledge of their behavior has dramatically increased the consistency and profitability of my investment decisions. This is not an insignificant relationship. The future will prove me right. Your investing profits will soar when you can

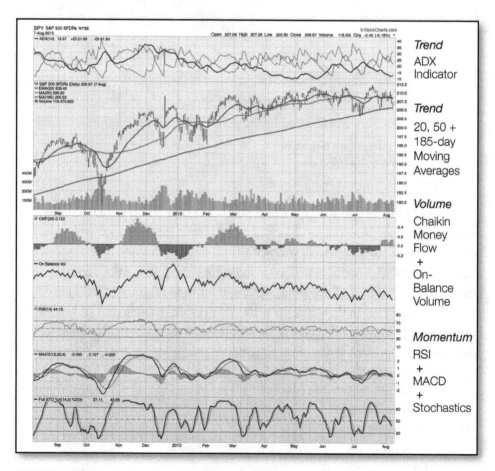

FIGURE 4.3 Market Analysis Indicators
Source: Chart courtesy of StockCharts.com.

put aside your desires for or preconceived notions about the present market, take control of your investor self, and place complete trust in your 10 chosen indicators. The market will speak to you through these indicators, and it will not lie to you if you are able to listen with an unbiased ear. Cultivating this ability takes time and will not happen overnight, but I assure you that it is a pursuit worth your focus and energy.

Although not fully weighted as one of the three essential elements of my methodology, I do blend technical analysis with some fundamental analysis and look closely at earnings-related data in addition to the primary technical indicators I have described. We will cover this in greater detail shortly in a later section of this stage. While my character lends itself more toward technical analysis of the market, your character may differ and lend itself more toward fundamental analysis. Whichever direction you lean, I encourage you to find the balance between technical and fundamental analysis that suits your personality and investment methodology. I refer to this mix as *rational analysis*. Together, technical and fundamental tools form a powerful combination that will fuel your trading performance and put more money in your pocket.

In total, these three elements of my methodology work synergistically to increase my probability of consistently making successful trades. By carefully laying out your own methodology, writing it out in your trading plan, and developing the discipline to adhere to it, you will place yourself far along the road to becoming a successful investor. Investment wisdom begins with the personal acknowledgment and acceptance of the fact that no one can predict the stock market with 100 percent certainty or consistency. A logical, personalized investment methodology, however, will significantly swing the probabilities in your favor and bring you closer to a personal mastery of the markets.

You may be familiar with the concept of *life hacking*, a term that refers to any productivity trick, shortcut, skill, or novel method used to increase productivity and efficiency—anything that solves an everyday problem in a clever, nonobvious way. When I first became familiar with this concept, I asked myself how I could embrace it as an investor and incorporate it into my trading. For our purposes, I will label this *investor hacking*: Individual investors achieve productive equilibrium by leveraging and utilizing only those tools they feel comfortable using and intuitively understand. This is to say, you should trade only those markets and time frames that are most appropriate for your lifestyle and allow you to remain emotionally grounded. It is crucial that you employ an organizational analysis that accommodates your level of discipline and available commitment. In essence, weaving all this together into a personalized trading system brings calm to the chaos of investing.

Having witnessed this in thousands of my investor students, I maintain that bad habits and poor discipline are the result of choosing inappropriate tools, time frames, markets, and organization methods. The reality is that optimal productivity flows effortlessly out of personal enrichment. Investor hacking is all about understanding your specific skill set and leveraging your talents to achieve a personal equilibrium, out of which profitable trading habits can bloom. It is, therefore, a requirement that you customize the methodology and routines I have presented to you to make them entirely your own, calibrating them to feel just right for you.

■ Organizing Your Analysis

As with so many other items in life, technology has been a true game changer in the financial industry. The tools available to us as individual investors in today's online world have given us a greater understanding of the global economic landscape and better access to the worldwide financial markets. Perhaps most important, these tools have dramatically improved our overall investing capabilities, allowing us to trade more like the pros on Wall Street. In the pre-Internet era, the greatest strength of professional money management was that the institutional money managers overseeing your invested capital had access to information and resources of which you as an individual were completely unaware—let alone able to use in your own investing. Today, however, information circles the globe in a matter of seconds, and the distinct advantages those institutions had in resources have been all but eliminated.

One of the most powerful developments of the past few decades has been the tremendous advancement of data management software, which has dramatically improved the organizational capabilities of the modern individual investor. When I first began investing, the Internet was many years away, and the conveniences it would eventually bring were nothing more than a fantasy. The markets I followed, the charts I studied, and the positions I owned were all on paper, clipped or copied and organized into physical folders in a file cabinet next to my desk. While that same conceptual structure still exists in the way I organize my investing routines today, the file cabinet has been replaced by a server far away from my office, and the manila folders have been substituted for digital ones. Though they're identified using many different names, we see these investment folders now on nearly every website that allows you to create an account—from news sources such as Yahoo! Finance to brokerages such as Charles Schwab. StockCharts.com calls them ChartLists; Bloomberg calls them WatchLists; Morningstar calls them Portfolios. While the vocabulary differs across platforms, the underlying function remains the same. These customizable, online lists allow you to add multiple stocks, funds, indexes, and whatever other financial instruments you are currently watching, assign a name to the list, and save it to be reviewed as frequently as you please.

As I will cover over the course of the next few stages, my analysis system and actual investing process both rely on an organizational structure that utilizes ChartLists heavily. Given my inclination toward charting, I personally have chosen to use the list system online at StockCharts.com. Moving forward, I will apply its terminology, but understand that I am using the word *ChartList* as a stand-in for the general concept of the customizable online list. There are many other website and software programs you can use in the exact same way. Again, while the names may differ, the underlying function remains virtually identical.

Here's the key: the collection of ChartLists I have named and populated with various indexes, ETFs, mutual funds, and stocks allows me to come into the office each day, log into one account, and quickly run through a broad-reaching yet in-depth summary of the current market action. Instead of having to search for each of the securities I wish to look at, each is right there in front of me, preformatted and arranged just the way I like it. Each stage of the Tensile Trading program from here on out has its own collection of ChartLists that I watch. I have a specific series of ChartLists that I use in my market analysis routines as well as many additional lists that cover the later stages of stalking, buying, monitoring, and selling. We will review these in greater detail in the upcoming stages, but for now, let us take a closer look at the ChartLists I review for market analysis on a daily basis. I do not suggest that you mimic these lists exactly in your own market analysis system; instead, my hope is that by looking over my shoulder at the routines that work for me, you will have a better understanding of how to build and organize your own analysis routines.

The very first ChartList I watch is quite broad. It provides a wide-angle look at the markets by covering four very standard U.S. indexes—the Dow Jones Industrial Average, the S&P 500, the New York Stock Exchange, and the Vanguard Total Market Index (VTI), which represents the entire investable U.S. stock market, including large-, mid-, small-, and micro-cap stocks regularly traded on the New York Stock Exchange and the Nasdaq. The fifth and final component of this first ChartList is the MSCI EAFE international index, which captures the combined performance of the major international equity markets as represented by 21 indexes from Europe, Australia, and Southeast Asia. This index simply gives me quick glimpse at the state of affairs in the world outside of the United States.

Next, I have an ETF-focused ChartList that consists of the 100 most heavily traded ETFs in the current market. To ensure that this list remains up-to-date, I rebalance it every quarter. By watching the money flow of these 100 funds and taking note of both the funds that fall out of the top 100 and those that move up into it, I am able to gain an accurate picture of how and where the big money is currently moving. My third ChartList is concentrated specifically on the international indexes. The funds in this list allow me to compare the performance of US equities to the rest of the globe and help me track which world markets are currently in favor.

Utilizing the top-down analysis method I discussed previously, my next step is to drill down from the market level into the major sectors of the US equity market. Vendors dissect the market using their own unique sector breakdowns with different names, but they all accomplish the same general goal. I have chosen to use the S&P Select Sector SPDR funds, which I group together into one ChartList. This list allows me to quickly analyze and compare the daily performance of each market sector. Digging down one level deeper, I do the same thing for the Dow Jones industry groups. Remember, different institutions divide the market in different ways. The Dow Jones has segmented it into approximately 100 industry groups, which I have compiled into a single ChartList. Similar to the sectors list, my industry groups ChartList allows me to quickly analyze and compare the daily performance of all industry groups within the market, giving me a more specific understanding of the current investment landscape.

Next, I have created two ChartLists for each individual sector ETF. The first includes its respective industry groups, allowing me to see which divisions are performing best within each sector. The second list includes the top 10 holdings of the sector ETF. For example, I have a specific list for the Sector SPDR Technology Fund (XLK), which is populated by the 10 largest individual tech stocks within that fund (note that the list of each fund's holdings can be found using a quick online search or on the SPDR website, www.spdrs.com). These 10 equities account for a massive percentage of the technology sector ETF. Because the performance of the fund is directly related to the price action of its specific holdings, I am able to gain a better impression of how the tech-sector ETF is likely to perform by further analyzing its largest individual stock components.

As I mentioned before, I am by no means suggesting that you copy these lists exactly in your own market analysis system. Over many years of experience, I have created a method that works well for me. As I continue to elaborate on this system in the coming stages, you will begin to see just how essential this organization is to my investing process. My hope is that by revealing the details of my system to you, your own development process will be greatly accelerated. I believe, however, that there is tremendous value in experimenting for yourself and discovering the structures, routines, and resources that are most ideal for your specific investor self. Take what I have presented you with here, and use it as a source of inspiration—a catalyst to construct your own organizational framework.

■ Common Misunderstandings

Throughout many years of teaching, I have noticed a series of common misunderstandings among my students. As they set out on their personal investing journeys, these misunderstandings can quickly turn from small confusions to dangerous and expensive mistakes. Many believe that there is only a single best method for trading the stock market successfully, a secret formula with exact and specific details to be uncovered. In truth, there are millions of successful methods. If you walk into your local department store, you see hundreds of pairs of jeans, each designed for a different shape, size, and fit. As the consumer, you are not searching for some magical pair of pants that fits everyone perfectly. Instead, you are searching for the pair that fits you perfectly. The stock market is no different. What is important is not the exact details of the method you choose, but rather that the method suits your personality and investment style. When an investor attempts to buy into a canned investment system they have pulled out of a newsletter or an article online, they will undoubtedly fail, because they lack a deep belief in the system and have not tailored it to fit their own investor self. Developing your own methodology should be an exciting and enjoyable process that makes you feel proud and accomplished. This sort of personalized preparation will give you the faith you need to trust your methodology through the emotional highs and lows of the market and will give you the discipline to stay focused and consistent in its execution.

In addition, many new investors believe that poor trading systems will succeed with good money management, but this could not be further from the truth. Every system must have an edge to it, something that gives it a spark or an advantage. The reality is that your own investor self is a significant contributor to that edge. Unlike many other skill-based activities, an individual without any training can be successful in the stock market for a short time simply by virtue of fortuitous timing. When this luck runs out, however, these investors are left with a treacherous overconfidence in their abilities and a virtually nonexistent trading system. The preparation necessary to construct a solid trading plan is time consuming and requires a significant commitment of physical and emotional effort. Once this foundation is built and the skill is mastered, however, the trading process becomes easier, the profits become more consistent, and the hard work you have devoted to investing produces benefits in the form of both market returns and decreased personal stress.

Many new investors jump into investing with the impression that to master the market is to always know the answer to why everything is happening. After all, educated people are, for the most part, trained to ask why. Professions such as engineering, law, medicine, and accounting invariably hinge on their practitioners' need to know exactly why certain things happen so they can generate solutions to complex problems. The assumption is, of course, that knowing why will ensure that all necessary information is gathered and that the most correct decision is made. While this strategy works brilliantly in these professions, the domain of the stock market is entirely different. In the financial arena, there is no promise of reward for understanding the underlying reasons something has happened. On the contrary: pursuing rational answers within a seemingly strange or misbehaving market may generate an academically stimulating list of reasons, but it will not necessarily generate any financial reward. An investor's pursuit of answers will waste precious time and energy and stall reactions. As a beginning investor, you must learn to overcome your need to know the root cause of all price movements and sentiment changes in the stock market. Instead, your focus should rest on identifying what is happening and following these conclusions with the appropriate action. Learn to understand what is happening, and develop the discipline and risk-management skills to act decisively with this information, turning your attention to probabilities over predictions. Believe your eyes, not your brain, and act upon the what, not the why.

Finally, new investors often suffer at the hands of a psychological phenomenon known as the *paradox of choice*. Succinctly, this is the idea that, in a world of excess choice, consumers often experience decision paralysis at the hands of too many options, freezing up and failing to make a decision at all. Alternatively, they may be left dissatisfied with the options they choose, because they can imagine a limitless number of other possibilities that could have made them incrementally more happy. From an endless number of investment websites to an infinite number of portfolio solutions, trading the stock market offers no relief from the paradox of choice. Novice investors often fall victim to this phenomenon and fail in their investing as a result, because they believe that to trade effectively is to exhaust all the information options available to them. Don't allow yourself to be swept up in the endless sea of resources to which you have access. With efficiency and execution in mind, you will find success by choosing a carefully selected basket of tools, resources, and indicators and intimately learning how to properly apply them to the particular slices of the total market pie on which you intend to focus.

■ The Market Stages and Technical Analysis

For those of you who do not recognize his name, Richard Wyckoff was an influential investor and stock-market educator in the early 1900s. Later in his life, Wyckoff turned his attention almost exclusively toward education and writing, and his works from this period in his life still offer tremendous wisdom for many investors today. Amazingly, the institutional buy-and-sell campaigns he exposed 100 years ago have stood the test of time and are still alive and well today.

Personally, Wyckoff's work has had an extensive influence on my own investing. My early studies and implementation of his *composite operator* model formed the basis for the methodologies and strategies that I developed and use today. Wyckoff's composite operator represents the market

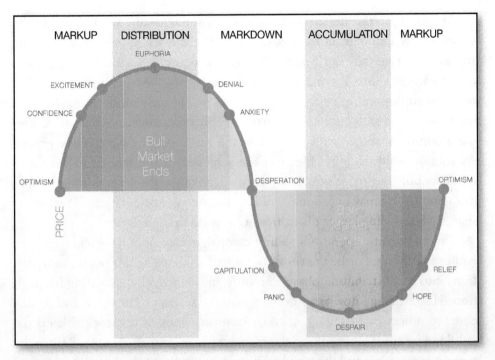

FIGURE 4.4 The Market Stages

methods and campaigns used by large institutions. In today's market, these are firms such as Fidelity, BlackRock, and Goldman Sachs. His model dissects the market's four cyclical phases—accumulation, markup, distribution, and markdown—offering insight into how the market is being traded by the major firms. He uses this information to fully understand the waves of money flow and properly time and execute investments. Figure 4.4 provides a visual explanation of this concept.

During the accumulation phase, the composite operator's objective is to buy specific stocks without advancing the price, thereby giving the appearance of liquidation or, at the very least, the apparent absence of buying. This discourages others from buying the stock and makes it seem weaker in the eyes of the common investor. This careful buying occurs until the supply has been soaked up. Now the strong hands represented by the composite operator—large investment institutions—have shaken out the weak sellers and absorbed their stock. The composite operator prefers to accumulate his line of equities in this manner, while the market is weak, dull, inactive, and depressed. He will often endeavor to scare shareholders out of positions by creating violent downward moves, known as shakeouts, or boring them out by forcing a stock sideways for long periods of time. In essence, he has put together a strategic buying campaign, one he will execute over time. He will continue to test the lower trading range of the equity's prices by strategically buying and selling his shares until he is convinced that all sellers have been exhausted.

At this point, the stock will have been moved from the weak hands to the strong hands, and with an absence of sellers in the market, even small demand spikes will drive the equity's price up. As the equity price turns upward and the stock shifts into the markup phase, the composite operator has control over the supply and can begin to let prices be bid up with demand. He uses his powers and influence to encourage good news and create positive media attention that spurs investment in the now seemingly attractive equity. As volume builds and his objectives are achieved, at some point he begins to liquidate portions of his position—very selectively, so as not to kill the stock's momentum. He may occasionally bid up and support prices himself by buying shares while selling larger quantities on upward price bulges.

The composite operator's selling campaign may either coincide with an equity's peak price or be the result of his exit strategy. At this point, he transitions into the distribution phase, carefully and selectively liquidating his position. His challenge now is to do so without depressing the price and to discourage others from selling, thereby ensuring enough demand to keep the public hope afloat and prolong the markup for as long as possible. Before the market turns down and the true bad news hits the public, he liquidates his final round of shares and converts his stock holdings to cash.

The market now enters the markdown phase as supply exceeds demand and prices start to fall. The composite operator has liquidated all his long positions during the distribution phase—before this downturn occurs—and shifts his portfolio into the appropriate short positions. As the grand manipulation comes full circle, he begins encouraging negative news and media attention to promote the drop in prices. Weak-hand shareholders—individual investors—are shaken out as they lose hope and sell their stock into the downtrend, and the composite operator either holds his portfolio in cash or maintains his short positions until the market eventually bottoms out and he can enter into another accumulation phase.

Time and time again, I have watched these cycles repeat and have seen Richard Wyckoff's insights materialize in front of my eyes. As individual investors, we are trading in the same market environment as these major institutions but without the exceptional market-maker power that they command. Our trades lack the immense volume necessary to move markets and shift the tides to our liking by buying or selling, and we are left with no choice but to ride the waves that flow in our direction. In many ways, today's stock market is identical to the markets of Richard Wyckoff's era. The players may be different, but the human emotions that drive the financial markets remain the same.

One thing has changed, however: the tool kit available to us as individual investors. Thanks to the glory of technology and the power of technical analysis, institutional investors can no longer hide their actions or intentions from the rest of us. In my experience, modern charting methods and visual analysis have shattered the effectiveness of the great Wall Street disinformation machine. The composite operator may still be promoting bad news and attempting to manipulate prices, but the charts give us instantaneous volume-accumulation analysis that allows us to track his real money flow and see through his smoke and mirrors. The speed of information in the Internet era is faster than ever, and price charts give us instant access to data in a manner not achievable with the ratios and figures of common fundamentals. Technical analysis has also improved our ability to use history to our advantage, allowing us to peer into the past to better understand the present and the future. As mentioned previously, times change but human emotions remain surprisingly constant, and these produce the very same recurring chart patterns and price movements.

The charting styles of technical analysis allow you to quickly achieve a level of profitable proficiency that would take years to reach using standard fundamental analysis that focuses only on raw financial data. Technical analysis engages the power of your visual senses, which can be an exceptionally potent tool for filtering out the massive amounts of disruptive and inaccurate information you will come across. Most investors easily fall victim to their rationalizing mind, convincing themselves that the financials and fundamentals are close enough and that an investment now is the right decision. Charts do not lie, however. They keep you true to the actual market in front of you and minimize the influence of your rationalizing mind. At the end of the day, all of this contributes to a stronger and more dependable formula for profitable investing. In my eyes, chart analysis is simply more appropriate for the stock market of today, which continues to move faster and faster and relies ever more heavily on modern technology. Technical analysis has been instrumental for me as an individual investor, helping me develop the ability to replicate my success in the market on a consistent basis. It is with this historical evidence in mind that I encourage you to implement it in your own investment system.

■ Fundamentals Checklist for Stocks

I have pitched my support for technical analysis and the benefits of charting, but in the spirit of full disclosure, I also incorporate a four-point checklist of market fundamentals when analyzing new potential investments. This is in addition to the technical indicators on which I primarily focus.

First in this four-point checklist, I look at earnings. After checking for any major surprises in recent reports, I review the company's current quarterly earnings growth rate and look at both its earnings-per-share (EPS) ranking and its price-earnings-to-growth (PEG) ratio. Overall, I try to get a sense of the trend of the company's earnings and monitor whether top analysts are raising or lowering their projections for the next quarter. After earnings, I look more closely at the economics of the industry and the sector to which the stock belongs to determine the strength of its performance relative to the total market. Third, I consider the following four key ratios:

1. Return on equity
2. Gross profit-margin trend
3. Management's percentage ownership
4. Institutional percentage ownership

These ratios allow me to gain a more in-depth picture of an equity's performance and gauge how strongly its management and large institutions believe in that performance. I do so by assessing how willing these entities are to invest their own capital. Finding stocks or mutual funds that are strongly supported by these individuals and institutions can provide an extra degree of promise and security for an investment.

Finally, I take some time to read up on current news surrounding the company or fund, often determining the information that is absent from the charts of raw financial data, such as new products coming down the pipeline or recent changes in the firm's management personnel. This helps keep my impression of the company's performance just a bit more grounded. These select fundamentals, in combination with the observations I have gathered in my chart analysis, give me a complete and accurate picture of what is going on in the market, and they provide me with the edge I need to make profitable investment decisions—trade after trade, year after year.

◼ Fifty versus Fifty

As we come to the end of the fourth stage of Tensile Trading, I leave you with a hypothetical to consider: Imagine that a collection of 100 new investors is split into two groups of 50. The instructor for the first group spends five hours teaching his 50 investors about fundamental analysis. He discusses price-to-earnings and debt ratios and tutors them on the ins and outs of income-statement analysis. The instructor for the second group, however, spends five hours teaching his 50 investors about chart analysis. He discusses trend, volume, and relative strength, and trains them on recognizing historical chart patterns. At the end of the five-hour session, both groups are sent out into the world and told to begin investing using only the tools they have been taught during the five-hour tutorial.

One year later, all 100 individuals are gathered together, and the investment performances of the two groups are compared. There is not a doubt in my mind that the second group of investors—with their newfound knowledge of technical analysis—will have outperformed the fundamentalists in the first group. It can take years of intense study and careful observation to gain the understanding and experience necessary to successfully invest based solely on fundamental criteria. Particularly in light of expanding globalization and the economic interconnectedness of today's worldwide business environment, the intricacies of fundamental data are simply too great for the average investor to fully comprehend. Charting, however, offers a much more comprehensible way to look at the financial markets. According to elementary financial economics, all fundamental data should already be priced into the market and therefore be reflected in the price charts on which technical analysis relies. This gives technicians a leg up on their fundamentalist counterparts and makes charting a more time-efficient way to analyze securities.

Now, as I previously discussed, I don't allow my support for chart analysis to entirely usurp all other analysis methods. I rely much more heavily on my charting tools, but I always make room for the fundamentals in my analysis routines. As I mentioned earlier, there is immense value in a combination of the two systems. Together, they provide a more complete and diversified view on the true state of a stock's price, cutting through the noise to zero in on the unbiased reality. With this combined strategy in effect, I consider myself neither a technical analyst nor a fundamental analyst. Instead, I am a rational analyst.

Key Takeaways

- Stage 4 of Tensile Trading focuses on market analysis. While my methodology outlined here aligns with my own personal trading style and risk tolerances, it can provide a working model that can be easily tailored to fit your investment profile. You must ultimately devise an investment methodology that fits you properly and stick to it. I recommend focusing on three key elements:
  1. Permission to buy. Using chart-based modules I determine the most appropriate position in the present market (e.g., a buyer, a holder, or a seller).
  2. A telescope-to-microscope approach. To maximize your probabilities of success, start with a telescopic lens (monthly data) and fine-tune your focus down to weekly and daily time frames, eventually looking through a microscopic lens at minute-to-minute data.
  3. Charting indicators. You will benefit from choosing a core set of indicators and maximizing your understanding of them. I limit my collection of indicators to 10, all of which I know and trust. Use your core indicators to buy strength, not weakness, and find industries, ETFs, mutual funds, and stocks that are outperforming the market.
- Embrace Richard Wyckoff's concept of the market stages. Use volume and money flow analysis to dig deeper into the buying and selling campaigns of the large institutions that control the markets.
- Finally, utilize an appropriate mix of technical analysis and fundamental analysis strategies. Combining the two into the stronger discipline of rational analysis will help increase your probabilities of extracting positive returns from the market.

Routines

In all walks of life, people ask the same question: What is the secret to success? I look around at our world, full of incredible and motivational stories, and I realize that we can glean invaluable investment lessons from exceptional individuals all around us. Often, looking in unconventional areas yields powerful insights and lessons that lead to more profitable investing. For example, I find it fascinating to watch world-class athletes—from Michael Jordan to Wayne Gretzky, Lionel Messi to Peyton Manning. Without exception, these professionals have made their greatness look effortless. Not surprisingly, the same holds true for great traders, who make successful trading seem natural. Reflected in the careers of countless other investors, I see displayed the same keys to greatness demonstrated by heavily decorated professional athletes. The fact is that those who have achieved mastery over their craft make greatness look easy.

As a young investor and a sports fanatic, I often asked myself why this was the case. In answering that question, I determined that these accomplished individuals focus on three elements. Similar to our earlier discussions on the importance of cultivating the investor self, exceptional athletes first look at how to minimize their failures by addressing their weaknesses. For example, if Tiger Woods decides there is room for improvement in his short game, then the putting green becomes his new home. Second, great athletes optimize the time available to them. Efficiency is a priority, and their workouts are structured to achieve maximum results in a specifically allotted time frame. Finally, once they have achieved a level of mastery, they learn to replicate their successes time and time again. In November 2013, LeBron James scored double digits for his 500th straight regular-season game. I aspire to this sort of consistency, which has become a model of success for me as an investor. With these three elements in place—minimizing their failures, optimizing their time, and replicating their successes—great athletes are able to purge their bad habits and replace them with new ones. They do so using high-leverage routines that deliver extraordinary results.

Having answered the question of *why*, I began to determine the *how*—how I too could achieve this level of mastery. Greatness came to these individuals I admired because they managed to jettison superfluous elements from their practices and implement the proper steps necessary to repeatedly succeed. In the stock market, the equivalent steps are specific, written trading routines, which form a roadmap for success.

Just as a winning sports team practices its playbook, so too must investors plan their routines and practice them regularly. Remember that these routines are nothing more than talk, however, without the cornerstone of profitable trading: discipline. Discipline is the lubricant that makes it possible to consistently execute your methodology day in and day out, replicating your successes and achieving mastery of the market. In the end, yes—you need the appropriate tools, a steadfast methodology, and effective organization to become a consistently profitable investor, but these elements are nothing unless cloaked in steady discipline. The simple truth is that, in the long run, an investor with the discipline to follow his or her routines will always earn more than an investor who bounces around and fails to exercise control. This being the case, maintaining undeterred commitment should be a primary objective.

I have come to realize that anywhere you witness the pursuit of excellence, you discover the same set of recurring universal truths regarding what it takes to achieve it. These are the cliché sayings your child's overzealous youth baseball coach probably loved to shout from the dugout: Practice makes perfect! Always give 110 percent! What it all boils down to is that great individuals manage to achieve mastery not simply because of raw talent but rather through years of intense, systematic, carefully planned training routines designed to maximize their improvement and maintain their peak performance. Just like an elite athlete following a regimented training plan, you as an investor must follow an equally regimented set of routines to maximize your performance in the market.

Choosing Your Time Frame

Have you ever met a successful investor at an event, taken his or her advice on a stock pick, and wound up losing money? If so, you are not alone. While it may have been a sensational and timely trading opportunity that netted the seasoned investor a healthy profit over a four-week period, perhaps you held the same stock in your portfolio for an entire year and came out deep in the red. Therein lies the crux of the investing problem: the exact same equity, traded over two different time frames, can yield shockingly disparate results. The undeniable reality is that we are all comfortable investing on different time horizons. While a conversation between a day trader, a position trader, and a long-term investor may be academically interesting, it very well may not be profitable for any of the three parties. They simply are not on the same page; therefore, they might as well be speaking different languages. Time matters on numerous fronts.

I believe our most precious commodity is time. Even the wealthiest person on the planet is restricted by the same 24-hour day as the rest of us. By crafting proper trading routines, however, I suspect I have effectively managed to squeeze 26 hours into each of my market days, thanks to efficiency. Formulating such a system can take a great deal of time and effort, but once you have completed it, it is astonishing how many charts you can review, how much information you can digest, and how many market landscapes you can cover when you are entirely focused and guided by an efficient set of routines. The two objectives of a well-crafted set of routines are to optimize your time and to maximize your observations, which together boost your efficiency and increase the effectiveness of your investing.

At the same time, realize that despite the effectiveness of your routines and regardless of how hard you try, the stock market is always one small step ahead of you. Think of the market as the rabbit on the rail at the greyhound racetrack. This is the bait set to run ahead of the racing dogs. As an investor, never mistake yourself for the rabbit. If you do, the market will humble you and remind you that you are, in fact, a dog. The best you can expect is to be a greyhound in close pursuit. After all, the market rabbit is not really in the race. Instead, you are racing your fellow greyhounds, who are the other investors on the track. These are the ones you want to stay out in front of, all the while keeping a close eye on the rabbit ahead.

In developing your personal investment formula, you must first determine how you will stay tethered to the market rabbit, and then determine how closely tethered you actually wish to be. Ask yourself what you are willing to do each day to maintain your connection to the market. Your personal daily circumstances, emotional commitment, and level of discipline should help you generate an honest and reasonable answer. With those inputs, you can then decide whether to allocate one hour per day or one hour per week. The difference between those two levels of involvement is not insignificant, so don't make the mistake of undervaluing the task of determining your most appropriate trading time frame.

Your time allocation must be unique to you. An increasingly significant commitment of both time and emotional capital is required the more closely you follow the market. Day traders, for example, must understand that the rope connecting them to the market is exceptionally short. This rope is longer for a position trader and still longer for a long-term investor. Realize too that there is no magical tether distance; depending on your personal circumstances and your investor self, any one may be appropriate for you. The challenge is to construct individual routines that work for your personality and your chosen trading parameters. By correctly matching your routines to your appetite for trading, you will remain in equilibrium both emotionally and physically. This will allow you to maintain consistent focus and discipline throughout the time you spend tethered to the market rabbit.

■ From Salesmen to Stock Traders

At its core, a salesman's objective is to convert potential buyers into committed clients. This simple model can yield powerful insights as to how top traders convert portfolio candidates into profitable returns. Truly accomplished investors know that a successful trading plan includes money management rules that accommodate both right and wrong scenarios—for example, by including a sound, protective stops strategy that addresses both bullish and bearish market climates. These investors' trading plans blend both elements so they can operate in harmony with the laws of probability. Both salesmen and investors know that when results become statistically predictable, they can be replicated more easily. Buying into this concept by factoring the bullish and bearish probabilities into your routines and your trading plan puts reality on your side and lessens the emotional toll of executing whichever strategy the market calls for.

As a hypothetical scenario, consider Frank, a salesman for the sandwich-shop franchiser Subway. Frank sells franchises to new owners who can afford to invest something north of $100,000 to start a new business they can call their own. To secure the sale of one Subway franchise, Frank must start with hundreds of potential franchisees. Phone calls to these hundreds of potential buyers yield perhaps 75 first-stage follow-up meetings, which in turn lead to only a few second- and third-stage meetings. Over time, Frank's preliminary search is winnowed down until it culminates in the successful sale of one new Subway franchise.

This scenario is a predictable game of numbers, a statistical exercise that functions in accordance with the laws of probability. The better and more experienced Frank becomes as a salesman, the stronger and more focused his sales routines become and the more he understands where and how to allocate his time. With this change, Frank increases the probability he will turn a regular and predictable number of potential buyers into committed franchise owners. Likewise, a stock trader earns predictably greater returns as his or her routines and trading plan become more refined.

Frank respects the advantages of diligently following his sales system; he knows that if he pushes an inappropriate deal or incorrectly forces one piece of the puzzle, the entire picture can crumble. For a trader, similar consequences result when you ignore a routine or impulsively rush into a weak trade. Just as Frank knows that his highest probability of selling a franchise comes when he explicitly follows his sales routines, traders who have the discipline to follow their trading plans with equal diligence and care are rewarded with higher percentages of winning trades. It sounds simple, and it really is that straightforward.

For Frank, a potential franchise buyer that does not result in a sale is somewhat predictable. He expends time and energy on the sales effort, but the loss is nothing more than the cost of doing business. He knows that he must move on, both physically and emotionally, to the next opportunity. Frank does not waste all day with a client he believes is unlikely to buy a franchise. The laws of probability require him to remove himself from any low-probability sales situations as soon as possible and focus instead on winning his next successful sale. By moving on, the probabilities place Frank one step closer to his next successful sale.

Now consider a top trader. This person risks time, energy, and capital in much the same manner that Frank risks time, energy, and money on a potential client. Like Frank, the trader cannot dwell on losing opportunities, because this wastes time, energy, and capital. Instead, he or she must deliberately move on so that he or she can focus on the next winning trade. Both the wise salesman and the profitable trader aspire to follow their respective system in pursuit of profits, and both remain positively motivated because they acknowledge the laws of probability and use them to their distinct advantage. Experienced traders know what a high-probability trade looks like early on. If an equity fails to behave like a winner, they cut their losses as quickly as possible. These investors follow their routines with discipline, subscribe to the laws of probability, and embrace the idea that each loss brings them one step closer to their next big winning trade.

■ Personal Peak Performance

Before I share my specific routines, remember once again that you will need to adjust them for your own personality and schedule constraints. Ask yourself: When are you at your best? How much time can you allocate to your routines? The answers to reflective questions such as these should shape how you formulate your personal investing routines.

First and foremost, recognize that each of us is most productive and effective at a particular time of day, and this time can vary greatly by individual.

Knowing myself as well as I do, I acknowledge that I am at my sharpest early in the morning; by the evening, I am clearly less productive. Grayson, however, is the exact opposite. He finds that his most productive hours of the day often come later in the afternoon and into the evening. No matter what your own reality is, recognizing and accepting the truths of your own body clock will profoundly impact your ability to maximize productivity.

Additionally, each of us has our own limits on the time we can allocate each day to our investing efforts. In my teaching career, I see overeager investors naively declare that they will allot five hours each day to investment management. At the other extreme, I see overconfident investors foolishly expect that they will need no more than just a couple minutes per day. Inevitably, both groups fail because they do not accurately assess their personal schedules in this early step. Most important is determining the amount of time you can consistently devote to your investing each day without deviating excessively. With a proper understanding of both your personality and your schedule, you will ensure that your investing routines are optimized for your investor self.

■ Daily, Weekly, Monthly, Annually

We have discussed in relative generalities the importance of routines in cultivating profitable habits and executing a successful investment methodology. I have also hammered home the idea that the most efficient long-range strategy for trading the stock market is to follow established routines of analysis and action on a consistent basis. Following these routines facilitates your personal growth as an investor and contributes significantly to the development of your market intuition. It will also help prevent dangerously impulsive or emotionally charged investment decisions by keeping you honest to your investor self. In addition, it allows you to better understand the factors that contributed to either a profitable trade or a loss.

My routines during premarket, market, and after-market hours and the time I allocate each day to weekly, monthly, and annual tasks center around my need to know precisely what is happening in the markets and among my positions. Note that this is a need to know *what* is happening, not *why* it is happening; the two aren't mutually inclusive. While the structure of your own routines will depend largely on your trading style and the time you can realistically devote to them, our core objectives should match. Your routines should reflect the very same desire as mine: to know exactly what is happening in the market and in your portfolio. To begin, create a written checklist of action items to keep yourself organized and avoid overlooking or losing track of any important aspects of your trading plan. This is the start of an outline from which the creation of other, more specific checklists can be built.

It would be unreasonable for me to assume that my students and readers all expect to be full-time traders, as I am. Regardless, I think there is still value in sharing some of my specific routines. But first, a few universal points:

- To be an effective trader, you must have organized, written routines that are relevant for the current state of the market. You should follow these methodically and trust them beyond a shadow of a doubt.

- You must be honest with yourself with regard to your other time commitments. Determine a manageable amount of time that you can and will devote to your routines each day, week, and month.

- If you cannot realistically allocate a small amount of time to your investments each day, then your routines should be designed to be completed on a weekly basis, at minimum.

- Assuming you can allocate some time on a daily basis, decide whether you will nibble away at your weekly and monthly requirements each day or will specifically choose one day per week during which you will address those items.

Daily Routines

- Examine the trend of the overall market.

- Check the price and volume behaviors of the major indexes (including the Dow Jones, S&P 500, etc.).

- Analyze market breadth by reviewing market participation levels.

- Check the daily money flow into the top exchange-traded funds (ETFs). (This will tell you where the institutional money is being invested.)

- Determine how the 11 S&P 500 sectors are behaving.

- Analyze which of the Dow Jones industry groups are the strongest and which are the weakest.

- Analyze market sentiment. How is the volatility index, or VIX—commonly called the fear index—behaving?

- Look at daily scans for high-volume equities and price breakouts.

- Visually review charts of all the equities I am stalking.

- Spend time looking at every equity I own (without exception).

- Check stops, triggers, and alerts for the positions in my portfolio.

- Record my daily observations and market notes in my trading journal.

Weekly Routines

Personally, I find that the easiest way to accomplish my weekly routines is to nibble away at them each day in small chunks. This way, I am not left with an overwhelming, unaccomplished to-do list come Friday afternoon.

- Perform a more detailed analysis of the key indexes and their price and volume performance.

- Review allocations and address what the market is favoring: large-, mid-, or small-cap stocks? Growth or value? International markets or U.S. markets?

- Perform a thorough intermarket analysis.

- Review my permission-to-sell checklist, which contains long-term indicators such as unemployment rates and industrial production and looks at certain historically sensitive leading industry groups.

- Review earnings and fundamental data regarding my equities under ownership.

- Look at the interest-rate environment and the conditions of the bond market.

- Depending on what is happening in the Dow industries, drill down deeper into the appropriate Fidelity Select Sector funds to see what the big-name mutual fund managers are buying and how the sectors are reacting.

- Review all working lists of equities that I am considering and stalking.

Monthly Routines

I have a detailed annual to-do list that contains items such as my net worth reconciliation, certain retirement accounts, tax preparations, insurance reviews, and more. For convenience, I parcel these out across the 12 months of the year, so those make up a part of my monthly routines. Your circumstances will be unique to you, but I strongly encourage you not to procrastinate in determining a similar list of monthly and annual routines. Unless you do so, these items can quickly bunch up and negatively impact your daily and weekly routines as deadlines unexpectedly approach. By accepting responsibility for your monthly routines every week or two, you will prevent them from becoming a burden.

Each month, I run the Morningstar.com X-Ray protocol, which often highlights allocations I need to adjust. You enter all of your positions—stocks, ETFs, and mutual funds—and the program unbundles each to give you a total picture that allows you to inspect your true asset allocations. In my opinion, the monthly subscription fee is absolutely worth the service price, and I strongly recommend it. Check with your brokerage as well, since the Morningstar .com service may actually be included with your account.

I also review all the brokerage statements I have received with a fine-tooth comb. I generate my own proprietary reports on each of my accounts and their specific holdings. I perform a detailed review of my calendar and update my long-term plan. Do take my advice: if you fail to control your calendar, it will grow to control you. Finally, I dig into certain asset classes on a rotating basis and do a detailed analysis during hours when the market is closed. Remember, none of these routines requires the mind of a rocket scientist. They do, however, require a healthy dose of discipline.

In the end, your routine rules should be simple and straightforward, and the organizational tools you use should make complete sense to you. Focus on your key daily routines before moving onto your weekly or monthly ones. Let your charts tell you what the market is doing, and allocate your time according to what you see, not what you hoped to see. Minimize the time you spend reading articles from *Forbes*, *Fortune*, or *BusinessWeek*. These are often little more than bubble gum for the mind: tasty but with no nutritional value for your investing approach. This is especially true for hard-copy news sources, such as magazines, whose material is inherently dated by the time it is printed and distributed. Old news is useless to you.

Likewise, keep yourself from becoming addicted to minute-to-minute news on the Internet or television. Spend your time first on monitoring your positions, executing your plans, stalking potential trades, and reviewing your charts. Make efficiency a priority, monitoring your time with the same scrutiny you use to monitor your positions. With these rules in place, you will have the strength and emotional control to follow your routines successfully and achieve your investing goals.

■ A Day in the Life

Great trading is the result of years of consistent effort, disciplined routines, and time spent cultivating your market intuition. You learn to manage what is in your control, accept the uncertainty built into every investment, and quickly put behind you the inevitable mistakes, bad decisions, or losses you experience along the way. I have so far illustrated for you my routines in a general way, but I hope that in now sharing with you the happenings of my typical trading day in detail, you will gain a better understanding of their real-world application.

Living in Seattle, Washington, I am three hours behind the U.S. markets in New York, which open for me at 6:30 a.m. Pacific Standard Time. Given this time difference, I operate comfortably from my home for the first three hours of the day. My home office space is a mirror image of my office in the city, largely thanks to modern cloud-based computing technology. This familiar environment allows me to work effectively from either location. I wake up, flip on the television in my bathroom, and stumble into the shower, listening to the television to keep myself in tune with the day's general news. I brew a fresh pot of coffee, then venture upstairs to my home office and boot up my computer—still before the market opens—to check activity on the Nasdaq premarket pages and the international markets.

My carefully organized ChartLists and these structured morning routines allow me to quickly assess the state of the markets and analyze the present status of my positions. With these tasks completed, I can turn my focus to the larger picture of index, sector, and breadth analysis. Breadth gauges the extent of participation in the market, in other words, the number of equities that are participating in the market's trend. I have a ChartList dedicated to breadth indicators that includes the following five charts:

1. NYSE New Highs–New Lows (This chart shows stocks in the NYSE making new highs minus stocks in the NYSE making new lows.)
2. NYSE Advancing Volume–Declining Volume (This chart shows stocks in the NYSE with increasing volume minus stocks in the NYSE with decreasing volume.)
3. S&P 500 Percentage Stocks Above 200-Day Moving Average
4. Nasdaq New Highs–New Lows
5. Nasdaq Advancing Volume–Declining Volume

In addition to those five breadth indicators, I also look at sentiment at this point in the day. Sentiment attempts to measure the degree of bullishness or bearishness in a market. As the market opens, I look closely at its psychology, tracking volumes, price action, and the Volatility Index (VIX).

Common Wall Street clichés concerning the opening hour suggest that the retail market—individual investors—drive the opening prices by executing their trades before hustling off to work. This is essentially the weak hands either buying or selling into the strong hands, the institutions and market specialists. With this in mind, I am seldom active as a participant in the first trading hour. Instead, my mornings center on reviewing my charts and adjusting the alerts and triggers I have set. Since I am watching the market closely during trading hours, I tend to use soft stops as opposed to the hard stops you would enter in the market with your broker. With soft stops kept on my own list, I will often sit tight if my price is hit on light manipulated volume, or when prices move unusually fast with high volatility (for example, in the flash-crash scenarios that have become increasingly common, market makers have trouble pricing stocks, and bid-ask spreads expand dramatically as a result). This prevents my position from being stopped out against my wishes.

Two hours into market hours, I have been awake for three hours and read both *Investor's Business Daily* and the *Wall Street Journal*. With a firm handle on the current state of the market, I begin packing up for the 20-minute commute to my downtown office, where I don my investing cap and settle in for an active day. The first thing I see when I walk into my office is a mirror. Staring back at my reflection, I ask myself a simple question that demands a most honest answer: "Are you up to the challenge today?" On the occasional days when my response is "no," I tape a small red square to the corner of my computer monitor as a reminder to try not to make any particularly large or important decisions that day. On most days, however, I am chomping at the bit to dive deeper into the markets, but I have learned to take a deep breath and quickly scan the list of trading rules I have tacked on the bulletin board that hangs above my desk.

To ease into my routines, I gather momentum by breezing through my permission-to-buy checklist. This is a top-down paradigm designed to reinforce my present outlook of the markets, breadth, key asset categories, sectors, industries, and top-performing stocks. I look for equities that align across all these attributes to produce the highest-probability trades. I designed this checklist specifically for my daily routine, and I strongly suggest that you create a similar matrix of your own, one populated by your own priorities and objectives and that reflects your trading style. Once you have decided what to do, you can then decide how often you will do it. Some items clearly need your attention on a daily basis, but others do not change as frequently and would perhaps be more appropriately revisited on a weekly or even monthly basis. Making these distinctions is vital in optimizing your time and developing an effective system of routines you will be able to follow.

Having completed an in-depth market review, my focus shifts to the equities I already own. My attention to protecting my assets always takes precedence over the search for new investment opportunities, which comes later. To assess the ongoing strength of the positions in my portfolio, I designed a tool that provides powerful early-warning signals that prompt me to take some money off the table while also giving me the confidence to keep money *on* the table when necessary to let a winning trade run. I call this tool the *sisters strategy*. The concept is simple: I carefully watch other similar equities— *sister equities*—within a stock's industry group to gauge the overall health of that industry and gain a better understanding of my position's probable future performance. Quite often, a subtle weakening in the performance of similar stocks within the same industry group will be followed by an equivalent weakening of a stock that I have invested in. As such, tracking the performance of these other equities is an exceptionally effective warning system that enhances my decision-making capabilities.

For example, assume you have invested in Johnson & Johnson (JNJ). In addition to watching the stock's individual performance and that of both the health-care sector and the pharmaceuticals industry group to which Johnson & Johnson belongs, you research other equities within the industry group to find its "sisters," comparing factors such as market cap, product or service offerings, and historical price correlations. Within the pharmaceuticals industry group, you might determine that Pfizer (PFE), Merck & Co. (MRK), and GlaxoSmithKline (GSK) are suitable sister stocks. These equities will serve as Johnson & Johnson's family, and the individual performance of each should be evaluated carefully in parallel to the position you own.

As the saying goes, a rising tide lifts all boats, and the stock market is no exception. My own personal variation on this saying is that if one member of the family comes down with the flu, there is a strong chance the rest of the family will eventually catch it, too. The performance of Johnson & Johnson is directly tied to its sector, industry, and other comparable equities, and the sisters strategy provides an additional level of analysis upon which to better understand and monitor your primary investment.

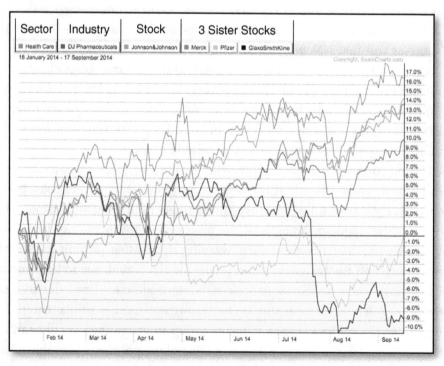

FIGURE 5.1   The Sisters Strategy PerfChart
Source: Chart courtesy of StockCharts.com

This sisters strategy works not only for individual stocks but also for mutual funds and ETFs. For mutual funds, sites such as Morningstar.com offer lists of similar funds that make it relatively easy to find sister candidates. The same concept applies to ETFs. I use other comparable ETFs as sisters, and I also track the performance of the top five individual equities that constitute the ETF I own. These are essentially part of the family, and they offer unique insights into the "mother" ETF.

Experience has taught me that a stock, mutual fund, or ETF levitating by itself, independent of its sector, industry, and sister stocks, is particularly rare. This sort of low-probability occurrence does not deserve my consideration as an investor. As such, the sisters strategy as I implement it is a primary part of my routine for every trade I make—while stalking, buying, monitoring, and selling. Routines such as these make it more likely that you can execute your analysis quickly, efficiently, and—for the most part—free from any dangerous love affairs or emotional attachments to the individual equities you decide to trade. As a result, you are more likely to invest based on the balance of evidence and reality you see displayed before you, viewing the market through a wide lens that captures more of the true market landscape and not simply a snapshot of one equity.

At this point, the trading day is approximately half over. I have a firm sense of the day's market pulse and am settled into my routines. My trading journal is open and available to me to note observations I make, key relationships I notice, and money flows I witness. My objective at this point is to remain mentally flexible and open to what the markets are telling me while keeping my emotions in check and executing my methodology. At this juncture I often find myself experiencing what I call the midday pause, a point at which I stop to reflect on my motivations and objectives and ask myself why I am trading the market. This becomes another opportunity to be brutally honest with myself and stay true to my methodology as I have written it in my trading plan.

As an investor, this sort of momentary uncertainty or self-questioning is inevitable in your trading. Anticipate it, embrace it, and cope with it. Your response to it is everything, and by calmly revisiting your own list of personal motivations, you can prevent it from becoming a disruptive force in your investing. I often take the opportunity to bring my trading journal to Starbucks, grab a cup of coffee, and take a brief step back from my immersion in the market.

For the remainder of the day, I become a juggler, keeping track of the multiple investment balls I have tossed in the air. I organize equities of interest—those that catch my eye—into one of the three categories in my stalking ChartLists, each of which is monitored according to its level of perceived urgency. My *buying* ChartList contains the equities I am taking new positions in as well as any existing equities in which I am looking to increase my position. My focus for these equities is on setting stops and percentage buying allocations while following current news and monitoring the weight of each equity in my overall portfolio. I tend to pull the trigger on new purchases later in the day, when liquidity increases and the bid-ask spreads tighten, but I am ready, willing, and able to do so at any other point if the evidence clearly presents itself.

My selling ChartList is the opposite of my buying list and contains the equities that I am looking to sell. My pyramid-out sales percentages and stops are listed here. We will define *pyramiding* in greater detail in Stage 7, but to summarize briefly, this is the process I use to buy into stocks, doing so in strategic percentages of the total position I intend to take. When it comes time to sell, I sell out of them in the same manner, according to specific percentages of the total position I own. In general, I am more aggressive in pyramiding out of my positions than I am when pyramiding into them. This acknowledges the reality that equity prices fall much faster than they rise. Although I always prefer to use limit orders (in which a trade is executed only at a price specified by me), I am more likely to use market orders (in which a trade is executed at the current market price) on the sell side, depending on price action at that moment.

The final market hour of the day is when the rubber really hits the road. This is when large institutions show their hand, which allows individuals to discern their true intentions. Volume analysis using minute-to-minute data—now easily accessible to us individual investors—provides the general population with what amounts to X-ray vision. It is virtually impossible for these major market players to hide their true buying or selling campaigns from us. Today, we have tools such as minute-to-minute on-balance volume, which allows us to see explicitly whether a stock is under accumulation or distribution. Think of volume analysis as the second hand on your watch. In my mind, trading without it is the equivalent of attempting to tell time using a one-handed clock: it's close but not very exact. With volume added in, my watch has a minute hand as well, making it accurate 100 percent of the time. Couple this insight on institutions' buying and selling campaigns with the fact that the end of the day brings higher trading volumes, and you can see why paying attention to the activity in the last hour of the day is so critical.

At this point, my desk and computer screen are clear of everything but the charts of imminent interest to me. I am ready to execute my methodology and set into motion either the bullish and bearish action plans I crafted during the calmer, closed-market hours. My computer screens are open to the appropriate brokerage accounts, which feed me live data from the broker I expect to use to place my trade. In this golden hour of market activity, my routines become my greatest asset, seamlessly guiding me through what can otherwise seem like complete chaos. Having sketched out my action plans beforehand and visualized their execution, I continually focus on remaining cool, entirely free from any outside distractions. The last 60 minutes of the trading day are my prime time, and I therefore treat them with the full extent of my discipline and concentration.

There is always more to do in any given day than the hours allow. Without a carefully crafted set of routines, the challenge of managing those infinite to-dos only grows. Being able to comfortably blend your working, investing, and personal lives into a collection of organized routines will offer a sense of control over their many moving pieces. This in turn facilitates confidence, a necessary psychological element of profitable investing. When you know what is next and you understand what to expect, you minimize stress and maximize clarity. To answer the question with which we opened this stage, that, my friends, is the recipe for success.

Key Takeaways

- Establishing consistent trading routines provides the structure you need to make the most informed investment decisions possible and achieve consistent returns. They minimize emotional challenges and impulsive trading while helping you develop your all-important market intuition. Like professional athletes, investors must embrace a structured plan of attack and remain dedicated to their trading routines. Daily routines should include examination of the market's overall trends and monitoring of all the positions in your portfolio. Each day, you should look at every item you own, assess the current state of your positions, and adjust your alerts and stops when appropriate. Record your observations in your trading journal to help you improve your discipline and remain focused on your investing goals. Proper routines can enable you to do this efficiently in just minutes.
- On a weekly basis, you should check your asset allocation percentages and review your long-term indicators and fundamental data for the positions you own. Perform a thorough review of key indexes, breadth, and intermarket analysis relationships.
- Your written trading plan should also include a monthly to-do list to keep up with other business-related matters such as retirement accounts, tax preparations, insurance reviews, and asset allocations. These monthly routines should break up your annual to-dos into manageable portions spread throughout the year.
- These types of structured routines ensure you don't find yourself caught off-guard or scrambling to get essential things done at the end of the day, the week, or the month. Every successful investor's to-dos or timeline will be different, so find those that allow you to complete everything in an efficient and effective manner within the constraints of your day.

Stalking Your Trade

There is a special art to the search for a winning trade, the process of methodically seeking out promising equities and checking them routinely for tradable opportunities. Finding and tracking the most promising and timely investments requires a keen eye and ample patience. Central to mastering the stalking process is embracing a specific investment focus. All securities—from stocks to mutual funds and options to commodities—are fundamentally different in how they must be evaluated and traded. The possibilities may seem endless, but this does not mean that your profits will also be endless if you can take advantage of them all. Rather than attempt to constantly cover all potential options, your trading plan should focus on a narrower and personally appropriate selection. Perhaps you choose three types of securities in which to invest, such as mid-cap growth stocks, exchange-traded funds (ETFs), and mutual funds. By adhering to this decision and maintaining your focus on these three, you will be more effective at stalking the investment opportunities they offer, and you will be able to do so with greater specificity and exactness. By staying true to your trading plan, remaining committed to the time frame you have determined is appropriate for you, and sticking to the security types with which you are most comfortable, you will increase your likelihood of consistently executing higher-probability trades.

Learning how to properly stalk a winning trade is a stage most investors transition through predictably as they evolve from novice to expert investor. Many novice investors have trouble limiting the number of sources from which they gather ideas—that is, instead of ordering from the menu, they flock to the buffet, where they become overwhelmed by the number of available options and end up overloading their plates. These investors are challenged again and again to winnow infinite choices down to a few promising candidates on which they can reasonably focus. Experts, however, have become disciplined in their practice of systematically stalking the markets. To continue our metaphor, they know their own taste, and they choose to order only the menu

87

items that suit it. They have carefully optimized their investment radar, and they know how to maximize the effectiveness of their stalking efforts. In the most basic market terms, expert investors have learned where to look, what to look for, and exactly how to look at the opportunities they discover.

◼ Where to Look

When a fisherman makes a successful catch, he records the coordinates of his haul. This allows him to return to its location later in hopes that another promising opportunity awaits. He's essentially journaling—and over time, this becomes a powerful and essential personal tool. For both fishermen and investors, history has repeatedly proven to be the best scorecard. As investors, knowing where to look should relate directly to our trading journals. The endless expanse that is the global financial markets can be nearly impossible to navigate. Your journal, however, limits the search parameters to something reasonable and encourages you to trade what you already know. After all, that is where your previous successes and highest probabilities lie. Although it may be exciting to invest outside your trading plan, doing so will in fact decrease your probability of long-term success. Very few professional hedge funds, for example, are able to execute a go-anywhere, trade-anything strategy with any consistency. Be selective in the sources from which you pull your investment ideas, choosing a manageable number that you can efficiently oversee.

◼ What to Look For

A watchful eye and careful logic will show you that the markets can be profoundly cooperative in showing you exactly what to look for. Well-designed alerts and triggers and computerized market scans can quickly winnow down your universe of candidate investments, offering a virtual cornucopia of fertile ideas and indicating the ideal time to buy a security you have been diligently stalking on both the long and short sides of the market. Whether you are scanning the markets for stocks making new highs, bullish technical formations, or specific candlestick patterns or are developing point-and-figure chart breakouts, financial scan engines do it all for you in a matter of seconds. These tools can be equally effective for finding bearish signals if short selling is what piques your interest. Perhaps most helpful of all, many online scanning resources have prewritten scan parameters. StockCharts.com, for example, offers more than 75 predefined scans that eliminate the need to write your own custom formulas; instead, they make the scan process as simple as a few clicks and a drop-down menu.

Given that my personal methodology is to trade on the long side, computerized market-scanning tools are exceptionally important in helping me find equities that are reaching new highs or breaking out of a trading range into a promising new uptrend. The new leaders of the market's next bullish move often spring from this pool. Having the right alerts, triggers, and scans in place and the discipline to remain vigilant will put you well out in front of such a move and keep you in the lead. For your stalking strategy to be effective, your methodology should be supported by a portfolio of watch lists, ordered according to priority, that you review diligently and as appropriate. My approach is to use three lists, organizing equities into a cascading flow from low- to medium- to high-interest items.

■ How to Look

Exactly how you look at an equity you have discovered matters, too. Novice investors may find this frivolous, but expert investors appreciate the value of beginning a trade by first centering themselves and reorienting their mind-set. Don't let the market's momentum or mainstream news get under your skin. Stay relaxed and rational, and remember that clarity of thought is your greatest ally. Purge your preexisting emotional baggage, and forget about your previous trades. Whether your last trade was a winner or a loser has no bearing on the possible trade at hand. Instead, each new investment must be judged solely on its own merits. In short, learn to stay true to your written trading plan and committed to your methodology.

At this stage, I look at equities primarily through the lenses of relative strength and money flow, utilizing the 10 indicators described in Stage 4. An intimate understanding of these tools has taught me to read and trust their signals, be they subtle, obvious, or somewhere in between. It is not a complicated tool kit of indicators—there is no need for extensive complexity—but it is *my* tool kit, and is supremely effective as a result. Read this sentence twice: you must develop your own stalking procedures based on a watchfulness, persistence, and focus and infuse them with a hefty shot of discipline and organization. At the end of the day, mastery is best achieved by practicing with the same basket of tools over and over again. By doing so, you will establish the muscle memory and intuition that together breed profitable investing.

■ When to Look

Financial markets are cyclical. They experience regular pullbacks, frequent corrections, and occasional recessions. Thankfully, for buy-side, longer-term investors such as myself, these weak periods of negative returns are not permanent. Recovery is inevitable, and markets always rocket back at some point down the line to take out previous price levels and move to new highs.

A recent financial report calculated annualized returns over an extended time period from 1995 to 2014 and found that, although the Standard & Poor's (S&P) 500 gained an average of just under 10 percent annually, the average individual investor returned less than 2.6 percent per year. With yearly inflation averaging around 2.4 percent, this means that the typical investor barely broke even. Previous iterations of that same report had in fact calculated even lower average investor returns—below the rate of inflation—meaning average investors were actually losing money each year.

While there are a wide variety of reasons for this underperformance by the average investor, one of the primary issues is that inexperienced individuals focus heavily on the short term and allow fear to dominate their investing decisions. Unfortunately, when periods of weakness strike and prices begin to tumble, most novice investors run for the hills. They pack up their cash; turn their attention away from stocks, bonds, and other securities markets; and ignore them until the good times return. I've even watched attendance at my investment courses shrink during recessionary periods, such as the period from 2008 to 2009 and the early 2000s. My behavior, however, and that of other experienced investors is generally the exact opposite: As prices fall, my ears perk up, my eyes open wide, and I turn my focus up a notch. I begin to assemble a shopping list of possible new acquisitions and review existing core positions that may be worthy of additional investment.

Downside pressures in a bear market environment drive the vast majority of security prices lower, but never in equal measure. To the astute investor, this can provide a clue. By using relative strength analysis to compare the performance of sectors, industry groups, and individual equities against a broader market benchmark—such as the S&P 500—you can determine the strongest stocks during the bearish climate. The top relative performers during a period of weakness often have a higher probability of becoming leaders in the next bull cycle, when the market eventually turns back up. Those are the securities I want to keep an eye on.

After a significant pullback, the market generally continues to shake weak investors out of their positions and intimidate or bore potential buyers, oscillating predictably within a trading range for several months. Market bottoms are rarely ever perfectly V-shaped. It takes time for the bulls to regain control as they play tug-of-war with the weakening bears. As prices move sideways over the course of this range-bound period, I work to identify the stocks that fared better than the market throughout the downturn and prepare to advance when the recovery sets in. I carefully craft a watch list of the stocks I am keeping close tabs on, and I make sure I am ready to spring into action when the uptrend resumes. Always remember that the greatest opponent you as an investor face is yourself. Managing your emotions, controlling your fears, and having the confidence, discipline, and patience to stick to your investment methodology throughout the good times and the bad will help ensure that, in the battle against yourself, the right you prevails.

■ Filters

In essence, stalking is the idea that it is your job to sift through massive amounts of data, information, and potential investment options to find the most promising and profitable opportunities. To stalk properly, you must create an information filtration system that can separate the good from the bad—the high-probability trade from the low-probability trade—to find the needle in the haystack. The filters you set to manage your stalking routines are your primary weapon against the great Wall Street disinformation machine. The markets continually generate ingenious techniques to test your patience, make you frustrated or mad, or bait you into doing exactly the wrong thing at the wrong time, even when in your heart you know better. Successful investors do not allow the markets to take them out of the game by getting under their skin, largely because they have developed effective filters to keep them operating on an even keel and protect them from the emotional roller-coaster ride into which the market so often drags inexperienced investors.

With this notion in mind, there are a number of primary filter categories that warrant your distinct attention: cost, price spread, and timing.

Cost

In the name of making money, your first filter should be cost. Your objective in investing is largely to maximize profit, so it is only fitting that you do what it takes to minimize items that otherwise diminish your returns. In addition to the necessary comparisons of cost and execution between brokerage houses—all of whom charge different amounts to execute trades—consider the supremely important cost differences between ETFs and mutual funds. Quite often, the very same mutual fund will be offered under multiple ticker symbols, all of which are associated with different fees and costs. This means that there may be many different ways to play the exact same fund.

Although the names in the following example have been changed out of respect to the managers involved, it uses actual cost figures for a real-world fund offered under four symbols. Let's call it the Pharaoh Connect Fund, whose four symbols carry the fees shown in Table 6.1.

TABLE 6.1 **Pharaoh Connect Fund Fees**

Symbol	Sales Fee (varies by broker)	Load	Expenses	12b-1 Fee	10-Year Cost*
AAAAX	—	—	1.63%	—	$2,105
BBBBX	—	—	2.38%	0.50%	$2,875
CCCCX	—	—	1.88%	0.75%	$3,050
DDDDX	—	5.75%	1.88%	0.50%	$3,050

*10-year cost based on $10,000 investment.

Looking at this example, and the 10-year cost in particular, you can see that if you fail to pay attention to the numbers, you would pay an extra $945 for the exact same investment—the difference in fees between the DDDDX and the AAAAX—all because you did not bother to complete the proper due diligence.

The reason these different tiers exist for the same fund is to provide compensation to sellers in various distribution channels. For example, a particular type of investment adviser may sell you DDDDX, because the 5.75 percent front-end load becomes that adviser's sales commission. Remember that if you invest, say, $10,000 in this fund, only $9,425 is actually put to work on your behalf in the market. Contrast that with an investment in AAAAX, which has no load or 12b-1 fee. Now the entirety of your $10,000 investment is working for you from day one in the market. Similar to front-end loads are 12b-1 fees, which in some ways can be more insidious. Brokerage houses will tell you that they are selling you a no-load mutual fund with no commission fee upon purchase, such as CCCCX. But the reality is that all or part of the 0.75 percent 12b-1 fee is paid to the brokerage each and every year that you own the fund. On a longer-term investment, this arrangement continues to take a bite out of your profits year after year. The lesson here is that staying vigilant with regard to cost minimization is an essential part of the stalking process. Without this focus, you can end up unintentionally handing away your hard-earned profits.

Price Spread

Along with cost minimization comes consideration of price spread. Stocks and ETFs have two prices that must be considered: the bid price (what you can buy the equity for) and the ask price (what you can sell the equity for). The difference between the two is known as the bid-ask spread, and it has very important implications for every investment you make. For example, say you are investing in a stock with a bid-ask spread of 30 cents. You purchase one share for $10, then immediately sell the share back. The market will buy it back from you, but it will pay you only $9.70 of the $10 you paid just a moment before. Understand that this means the stock must appreciate by 30 cents before your investment can actually break even.

This price spread reflects the underlying confidence that market makers have in the equity in question. For example, less volatile equities traded with large volumes will have very small price spreads—something along the lines of one cent. Highly volatile equities traded in lower volumes, however, are less inspiring of confidence and more risky for the market makers. They are therefore traded with high price spreads. This is a generalization, but by buying equities traded with high volume and low price spreads, your investment is likely to be more stable and secure compared with a highly volatile stock that trades sparsely within a wider range and at low volume. While I do not suggest that you buy only small-spread securities, ensure that you have collected all the relevant information and considered the alternatives before purchasing a new position. As you sift through the countless equities available to you, filtering them for high relative volume and low price spreads, simply make sure that you fully understand what you are buying. Remember that checking the spreads indirectly tells you the risk the market makers have assigned to that equity, and if price spreads are wide when you buy, you can assume that they'll be even wider when you go to sell.

Timing

Last, put a series of timing filters in place while stalking your trades in order to determine the most opportune times to invest. For mutual funds and ETFs, it is absolutely critical to look at distribution dates before buying even a single share. Buying into a fund just before a distribution date will result in an immediate return of your capital back to you in taxable form. Many investors unfortunately gloss over this very important aspect of investing and wind up making large and entirely unintended donations to Uncle Sam. Don't make that same mistake. Simple checklist items like this can put easy money in your pocket.

Distribution and Earnings Dates In addition to normal price movements, many stocks, ETFs, and mutual funds offer various distributions. These can be regular payouts, such as dividends, but occasionally they can also include capital gains and other special distributions. Dividends are predictable while the other distributions are less so, but both have significant tax consequences. If you choose to have your distributions reinvested rather than paid in cash, your bookkeeping procedures become supremely important. Historically, some derivatives-based ETFs have unexpectedly issued large, taxable distributions. These can easily catch shareholders off-guard, surprising them with a significant return of capital on which they have to pay taxes.

The crucial point here is that you check annual distribution dates from past years, because they can provide insights into what you should expect from a stock or a fund moving forward. When investing in a mutual fund—particularly over the intermediate or long term—the tax implications are especially critical. When you sell your position in a mutual fund, you pay capital gains tax on its appreciation during the time that you owned it. In addition, these funds offer distributions based on the long- and short-term gains made when the managers decide to sell individual equities in their portfolios. You are also required to pay taxes on these distributions, whether you elect to reinvest these in the form of additional shares or take them in cash. This is why bookkeeping matters.

After a distribution, the value of new shares that have been reinvested must be added to your previous basis to raise it to a new, higher level. When you eventually sell out of the fund, your position with the higher cost-basis level will reduce your taxable liability and minimize the capital gains tax you pay. This is just simple math: a higher cost basis means a smaller profit total, and a smaller profit total carries a lower capital gains tax. Unfortunately, investors all too often fail to appropriately recalculate and increase their basis to reflect reinvestment of distribution payouts. Because your basis determines the amount you pay in capital gains tax when you eventually sell the fund, this becomes an expensive mistake. Today, brokerage houses are required to update your basis for you, but from personal experience, their calculations are not always correct. As such, there is a great deal of merit in understanding how the system works and why this process is important.

Some years ago a student of mine paid the price for failing to properly consider historical distribution dates when he purchased the Fidelity Magellan fund (FMAGX) in May 2006. When he told me that he had purchased this fund, my radar went up immediately: I recalled that Robert Stansky had left his position as its manager in the year before. This was a shaky time to invest in the Magellan Fund, because the new portfolio manager, Harry Lange, was likely to move the fund in an entirely new direction. As projected, Lange sold a significant percentage of the fund's appreciated positions, triggering massive capital gains that were then distributed to shareholders shortly after my student bought in. My student had invested approximately $100,000 in the Magellan Fund on May 3 at a share price of around $65.00. On May 5, two days later, the fund declared a distribution of $22.36 per share, largely representing the capital gains that Lange incurred by selling the previous manager's appreciated assets. My student received approximately 34 percent of his investment back as a capital gain, which he was then forced to pay taxes on.

His mistake was in not checking Magellan's historical distribution dates, which clearly showed that the fund had a regular pattern of paying distributions in early May each year. Now cognizant of both distribution dates and the potential impact a manager change can have on a fund, he admitted that this was a mistake he would never make again. Unfortunately, he learned it the hard way. Although I have chosen this example for its shock value, it clearly illustrates my point: history matters. Before jumping on board with an investment, make sure you check the distribution dates to avoid suffering the downsides of a timing error.

Another essential element you must monitor closely—though it is not a distribution—is earnings dates. Your broker's website is an ideal resource for finding these dates and other pertinent details; alternatively, a quick Google search will reveal dozens of other reliable websites that provide this information. As a rule, I will not buy a stock prior to an earnings report date. There is simply no definitive way to tell what surprises might be in store when this information goes public, and volatility often escalates as a result. Earnings drive prices in the stock market, and without properly considering these critical dates, you can end up on the seriously wrong end of a bad earnings report.

Seasonality In addition to distribution and earnings dates, another helpful timing filter can provide a powerful edge for your stalking tool kit: seasonality. Earlier, I mentioned considering past historical evidence before trading. Nowhere is the cliché "history repeats itself" more true than in the financial markets. The reasons for this are many. Among academics, studies of behavioral finance have proven that although markets may change dramatically, human emotions have changed very little over the centuries, and they remain one of the primary drivers of the market. For a host of complex reasons relating to earnings, institutional money flow, and other factors, many equities trade in distinctly seasonal patterns and display clear historical trends, rising in certain months of the year and falling in others on a recurring annual basis. Fortunately, the seasonality tools available through many brokerage houses and other resources, such as StockCharts.com, can help you optimize your investments throughout the year on both the buy and sell sides of your trading. As an investor, it is to your benefit to use this concept to your advantage, putting the power of statistical probability on your side by buying in historically weak months and selling into strong months.

The idea behind seasonality is simple: It looks back at multiple years of historical data and averages price movements to determine the percentage of months in which an equity closed higher than it opened as well as the average price change for each month. Institutional investors have used seasonality to their advantage for many years, and now this effective market filter and timing tool has reached the public sphere and made available for individual investors.

Figure 6.1 shows an example of a five-year seasonality chart for PRFZ, a PowerShares small-mid cap ETF. As you can see, between 2011 and 2015, PRFZ closed higher at the end of February, March, and December 100 percent of the time, with average price increases of 4.2, 2.0, and 2.1 percent, respectively, per month. On the flip side, the fund closed higher at the end of April and July just 20 percent of the time, with average price decreases of

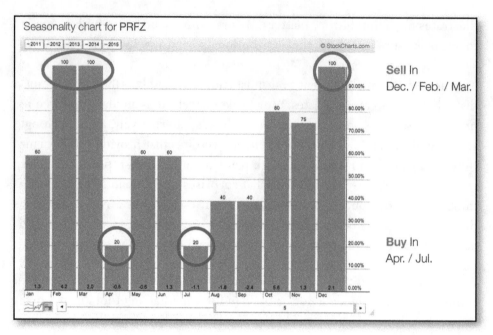

FIGURE 6.1 Seasonality Charting
Source: Chart courtesy of StockCharts.com.

0.5 and 1.1 percent, respectively, per month. With this information, history tells us to be a buyer at the end of April and July and a seller at the end of December, February, and March. My point here is simple: use these statistical probabilities to your advantage.

Seasonality is an exceptionally powerful accumulation and distribution tool. If you are accumulating a position over a number of months, it provides unique historical insights that can improve your timing. By clearly identifying periods of historical weakness, seasonality charts can help you buy an equity at a discounted price. On the flip side, if you plan to exit out of a long-term position, reviewing monthly trends and statistical data over various time frames can help you determine periods of historical strength into which you can sell. By helping you buy on weakness and sell into strength, seasonality will make you a more informed investor and quickly become the ace up your sleeve. Experiment with this powerful tool, and include it in your stalking arsenal. The addition it makes to your trading plan will further transform your investing routines and methodology into robust probability enhancers.

■ Human Nature and Overhead Supply

In Stage 4 and elsewhere, I have expressed my support for charting and visual analysis, and hopefully presented a convincing outline of why I believe it is the clearest and most effective method of analyzing the stock market today. In the

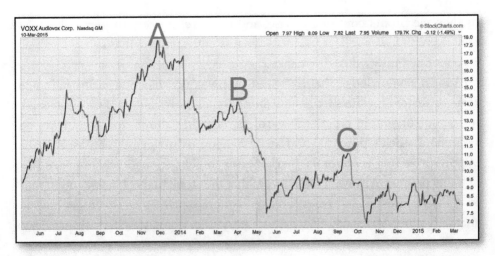

FIGURE 6.2 Overhead Supply
Source: Chart courtesy of StockCharts.com.

stalking phase of a trade, the power of these visuals skyrockets. For example, the chart in Figure 6.2 displays what is known as overhead supply.

Overhead supply acts as a probable ceiling that a stock's present price action must break through as it tries to move upward. In this example, investors who purchased this stock at point A bought at the top of its uptrend and lost money as the stock price fell significantly from its high of around $18 per share. Those who have held on to the stock have their fingers crossed and continue to hope that its price will rise once again, allowing them to close out of their position at a net of zero and without a loss. Having spent enough time on the emotional pricing roller coaster, the majority of these remaining investors will sell as soon as the stock's price once again rises near their breakeven level out of fear of future volatility. The same is true for the investors who bought in at points B and C. Both of these groups experienced significant losses after they invested in the stock, and they, too, will be eager to sell as soon as the price rises back up to that of their initial purchase. Together, these investors create what's called an overhead supply, which has the potential to dramatically diminish the strength of buying campaigns as the stock attempts to rise. As the stock price now tries to rise from its low of $7 and take out its previous high around $18, it has to work against pockets of eager sellers at points A, B, and C. Often, this makes it tough for a stock to regain new price highs or sustain a strong uptrend.

This sort of potential performance threat is clear as day on the charts, but it is not reflected at all in the raw fundamental financial data. This is one of many examples in which charts simply paint a clearer and easier-to-interpret picture of what is happening in the market and what is likely to happen moving forward. I prefer to buy a stock that is hitting a new high, because at that point, overhead supply has already cleared out. The remaining investors who own it are now patting themselves on the back and applauding their genius as they see profits continue to rise, and they are unlikely to join a chorus of sellers. With fewer sellers, chances are this enthusiasm will directly correlate to continued upward performance.

I must acknowledge that overhead supply concerns do typically fade with time; investors inevitably tire of waiting indefinitely, and so they often sell at a loss out of simple fatigue. Regardless, charting allows you to quickly determine a stock's potential and avoid dangerous patterns, such as overhead supply, providing yet another market filter to help dramatically improve your stalking process. Always remain aware that the stock market is an auction market. Prices rise and fall based on the economic principles of supply and demand. If supply dries up, even a small amount of demand will drive prices up.

◼ Second-Opinion Resources

In the days before online brokerage accounts, your stockbroker acted as a second opinion, a sounding board off of which you could bounce investment ideas. When you called your broker and asked to place a trade for 500 shares of Ford, he or she would discuss the purchase with you in depth, providing analysis of the market's current state, the stock's prospects, and the strength of your investment idea. Those days are mostly long gone, however, and the process of consulting with your broker has been replaced by a multitude of online resources offering in-depth analysis and ratings on every stock, ETF, and mutual fund you want to know about. While these services should not be your primary source of information or ideas, they often provide additional insights into and verification of an investment's potential—or they can reveal evidence that an equity is not the star trade you dreamed it might be. The opinions and earnings data offered by Web-based resources such as *Investor's Business Daily,* Morningstar, Nasdaq, and TheStreet can be valuable in determining what the professional-level consensus is with respect to an equity, as well as the analyst ratings and earnings trends for a particular investment. It is perfectly acceptable to use this information as a decision-making helper—the last swing toward either a go or a no-go. But again, remember not to let yourself become overly absorbed in these websites. What starts as a useful tool can quickly become a minefield of information overload and indecision.

◼ The Sisters Strategy Revisited

The stalking stage is a perfect opportunity to revisit the sisters strategy we discussed in Stage 5. This strategy is based on the fact that the financial arena relies heavily on groupings. As a reminder, sister stocks are similar stocks from the same sector and industry that can help provide a more complete picture of the segment or "group" of the market that supports an equity you are considering. As you research a stock of interest, you become more familiar with the sector and industry group and the equities that constitute them. If the industry looks healthy and is finding favor among institutional investors, your objective is to choose the best stock from within that group. Don't be surprised if this ends up being a different equity than you initially expected. In further researching your stock pick, identify some ideal sister-stock candidates to monitor alongside the equity you intend to target for purchase. Having researched both the industry it belongs to and its competitors within that group, you will feel more confident in deciding when and how much of your trading capital to allocate to the trade.

Once you own the stock, continue to monitor the appropriate sector and industry indexes, the stock itself, and several of its sister stocks. This will provide a broader, clearer perspective on the exact state of affairs in the segment of the market in which you have invested. We will address this in greater detail in Stage 8. When the market begins to tell you to sell, you will see the signals reflected in the deteriorating performance of both the industry group index charts and the weaker sister stocks that you have been monitoring. From here, based on mounting evidence of deterioration in the family, pulling the trigger on the sell side becomes a quick and easy decision to make. A similar approach to the sisters strategy applies when stalking and monitoring mutual funds and ETFs as well.

The one weakness of the sisters strategy has more to do with an individual investor's ability to choose the most appropriate sister equities than with the actual strategy itself. Novice investors must remember to consider companies from the same industry and of similar size, according to the companies' financials. Historically speaking, these sisters should be closely correlated to the primary equity with respect to the stocks' past price performances. The effectiveness of this strategy ultimately relies on initially choosing the most appropriate sister stocks, a skill that you will grow to perfect with practice. Your broker's website and others, such as Morningstar.com, provide many tools to assist you in this endeavor as well. Overall, this organized and reliable analysis method is a centerpiece of an effective, high-probability stalking approach, and when properly utilized, it will strengthen your entire investment process and improve your ability to consistently replicate your most profitable trades.

■ Mimic Wall Street's Masters

In most instances, the big gorillas on Wall Street have the upper hand over us individual investors. With massive capital reserves, a direct line to nearly every trading desk in the world, and the inside track on the latest information, the resources available to today's hedge fund and mutual fund managers are tough to beat. There is one unique and powerful advantage, however, that you as an individual investor have over the major players.

In recent years, a new breed of ETFs has emerged that mimics the top-performing funds on Wall Street. This is possible because regulations require money managers with more than $100 million in assets under management to disclose their holdings every quarter. Funds such as Global X Guru (GURU), for example, are able to assemble a basket of the stocks that are the most commonly held by a prescreened group of the most successful actively managed funds. The logic here is sound, but fortunately for us, we can execute it even better on our own.

Consider the financial giant Fidelity. This is an institution with more than 40,000 employees and trillions of dollars in assets under management. Of the big gorillas in the financial arena, Fidelity is just about the biggest. Fidelity spends millions each quarter on the old-fashioned, in-depth research for which it is internationally renowned, and it is required by law to disclose every three months the holdings that its fund managers decide to own. As these professionals begin their buying campaigns, we as individual investors can dig into their disclosed holdings for a closer look at where the smartest institutional money is flowing. As previously discussed, institutional support is often an essential element of price appreciation for any stock. With this in mind, what better place to look than a list of stocks most commonly held by top fund managers?

Given that Fidelity in particular is such a significant institution, I personally track many of its funds' holdings quite closely. Fidelity has 40 Select Sector Funds that are actively managed by some of the brightest minds and best investment teams in finance. These are highly influential mutual funds, with tremendous research teams that drive their decision making. I maintain a ChartList for each of these 40 funds, populated with the top 10 holdings of each. Every quarter, when the funds disclose their top 10 holdings on the Fidelity website, I update my ChartLists to reflect their current portfolio compositions. I take careful note of any stocks that have been added to the top 10 list and, equally important, any stocks that have fallen out of the top 10. When I notice that a stock appears in the top 10 lists as a new addition across multiple sector funds, I know that Fidelity is telling me, "Hey, we really like this stock!" Conversely, when I see a position falling out of the top 10 lists of multiple sector funds, I know that Fidelity's support for that stock is vaporizing. As you can imagine, betting against weakening institutional support from one of the world's largest financial firms is not the high-probability trade I am looking for.

The insights that this process provides are invaluable. Coupled with my trend and volume analysis procedures, this exercise gives me a powerful window into the current accumulation and distribution campaigns of some of the most sophisticated and well-researched funds in the world. The final call depends on what I see in my own market analysis, stalking, and buying routines, but by studying how and where the Wall Street masters are directing their capital each quarter, I am able to use them as my personal research team and close trading partner.

◼ The Base-Hit Investor

I was living in Seattle in 2004 when Ichiro Suzuki was crowned the Major League Baseball American League batting champion, with a batting average of .372. I have always found him to be an inspiration for me as an investor. He was never known as a home-run slugger but instead made a name for himself as an exceptionally consistent base hitter. In fact, in 2004, Ichiro hit only eight home runs. When I compare this to other superstar players, such as Mark McGwire—tenth on the list of most career home runs with 583 but with a batting average of only .263—my character as a trader leans more toward the impressively consistent on-base hitting of a player like Ichiro.

This comparison parallels my experiences both as a stock trader and an educator. After all, I have known many investors whose personalities align closely with one of these two very different baseball players. Those who emotionally align themselves with the slugger attitude of a Mark McGwire are big, bold extroverts, full of confidence and zeal. Often, they happen to stumble into the market just at the bottom of a major pullback. They execute a few home-run trades and then, lo and behold, are convinced that they have been endowed with a magical hand and are blessed with unique and powerful superhero trading skills. The challenge and the risk in this scenario is that, having drunk from the chalice of profits and tasted the sweet nectar of home-run success, they are often never again satisfied with a small base-hit victory in the stock market. The goal becomes the home run, and all attempts now swing for the fences, taking big risks in hopes of big rewards. Having never taken the time to build a solid foundation of investment knowledge or intricate planning, they do not understand how to book a gain or properly handle a loss. It is easy to be blindly tempted by the addiction of the big hit and fall into a downward spiral of home-run investing, especially for traders who lack in-depth planning and an understanding of the basics.

Contrast this with the Ichiro Suzuki of investors. These individuals are often more streetwise and less brazen. They are patient and shrewd. Analytical and rational, they keep their eyes on their long-term objectives rather than short-term payoffs. In place of the single hammer of the home-run investor, the base hitter's style is more akin to an automotive technician, who has a wide array of tools for specific jobs and careful expertise in maximizing their use. Risk is carefully balanced against reward, and the deliberate, calculated steps taken to achieve a more modest end goal take the form of small, consistent victories rather than a myopic focus on occasional home runs.

Ask yourself: Do you want to be in the business of hitting home-run trades, or are you better suited to the business of consistent hits that land you on base? With either option, your answer deserves an acknowledgment and a careful explanation. My suggestion is simply that you recognize your personal risk tolerance and understand the costs associated with wanting to chase the big reward on every trade. Personally, I have found that my investment enthusiasm is maintained and lubricated by regular base-hit investments and smaller, regular victories that together form a consistently profitable machine—but this may not be true for you. More important than the path you pursue is your acknowledgment of it and your ability to adhere to it over many years in the market. Doing so myself has helped my trading remain focused, kept my ego in check, and allowed me to succeed.

Key Takeaways

- Stalking is the disciplined art of methodically knowing where to look, what to look at, and how to look at only the most promising, highest-probability investments.
- You must limit your sources for trading ideas and deploy filters that can winnow the infinite universe of investment options down to a few of the strongest candidates. Remember that for a stalking strategy to be effective, it must be supported by an organized series of increasingly important watch lists, maintained and monitored regularly.
- Your trading journal is once again an important resource at this stage, allowing you to review what has and has not worked in the past and capitalize on the insights that your own experiences can offer. Stay true to your trading plan and focus on the time frame and security types with which you are most comfortable.
- Using filters to hone your focus is an essential stalking strategy. Costs should be one of the first filter criteria you apply; focus next on price spreads and timing your trade. Additionally, take advantage of alerts and triggers offered by your brokerage.

Buying

Since a young age, I have been a devoted car enthusiast. Most years in January, I travel down to the Barrett-Jackson car auctions in Scottsdale, Arizona. As I look around at literally hundreds of cars I wish I could buy, my heart pumps, my mind races, and I struggle to pick my jaw up off the floor. Despite these limitless desires, I am brought back to reality by acknowledging that I ran out of garage space many years ago. I have known many investors who view the stock market with a similarly overloaded excitement. Unfortunately, they fail to recognize the limits imposed by their own mental garage space, if you will. For them, buying equities is a joyful, impulsive expression of their present wealth. They park dozens—even hundreds—of stocks in their portfolio, just like the curator of a world-class automotive museum. Investing, however, is not like car collecting: It requires logistical planning, dedicated monitoring, and a specific exit strategy for each and every position if you hope to turn your time and energy into cold, hard profit.

When I am feeling impulsive and longing for a new car, I pull out my checkbook and pore over the balances. Similarly, when I am about to buy a new stock, I pull out my trading plan and review a series of key routines and procedures. My first step is to quickly flip through what I call my permission-to-buy ChartList, which forces me to look at present market trends, allocations (i.e., whether the market is favoring large-, mid-, or small-cap equities, growth or value stocks, etc.), breadth and volatility, and the current strength of the sectors and industries. If the charts indicate that the market is not giving me explicit permission to buy, then my finger quickly comes off the trigger.

A distinct benefit of this permission-to-buy review is the clarity that it brings to my outlook on the current market climate. It allows me to stay focused on the best-performing sector and the best-performing industry group within that sector. If institutional money is flowing into a specific industry, I want my own money to follow. Most individual investors do not fully appreciate the immense advantage we have over the institutional money managers, which is that—unless you are trading equities priced under $10 (most institutions forbid their portfolio managers from trading stocks below $10, due to liquidity concerns) or pink-sheet penny stocks—your trades will simply never have enough weight to move the market. In other words, your low-volume trade will be executed with little to no fluctuation in price.

The reality is that it is very easy to accumulate (buy) positions in $3 stocks, but when it comes time to sell, the small-cap market does not welcome sellers with the grace it does buyers. Prices tend to be much softer in stocks without any institutional support. This is most clearly reflected in the bid-ask spread, which can be unusually large. Selling 50,000 shares in a low-priced stock, for example, can easily lead to a sharp price decline, because the market simply cannot absorb the sort of volume it can in other, higher-priced equities, which are supported by institutional managers.

For this reason, individual investors too should generally refrain from fishing for equities below $10 unless they can sense serious institutional sponsorship or recognize the powers of accumulation occurring behind the scenes. On some occasions, I have seen stocks accelerate rapidly after crossing the $10 threshold, the point at which many institutional managers are free to launch their accumulation campaigns and begin buying. We, as individuals trading the market, can operate much like the little mouse that jumps on the back of the big elephant to enjoy a free ride. In our case, such a ride leads straight to the money tree.

Excitingly, the modern technical analysis tools we have at our disposal can clearly show us when the big elephant begins accumulating a specific equity. In particular, I encourage you to use Joseph Granville's On-Balance Volume indicator. When applied to a chart that displays minute-to-minute data—which is now widely available to us as individuals—it becomes impossible for big institutions to execute their accumulation campaigns without leaving large, distinct footprints.

Some years ago, my students and I owned the accessories designer Coach (COH) in our class portfolio for the semester. After a few weeks, the stock had slipped about 8 percent, which, understandably, left half the class lobbying that it was time to sell. The other half—myself included—sensed that there was something bigger going on in the background. Looking at a chart of the stock's previous 10 days using minute-to-minute data and tracking the On-Balance Volume indicator, it was clear that Coach was the target of a serious accumulation campaign, despite its relatively severe price decline.

Based on this divergence, I recommended to my students that we continue to weather the storm and hold the stock. Lo and behold, it was announced shortly afterward that Coach was to be added to the Standard & Poor's (S&P) 500 index, after which its price promptly doubled. Well before the formal announcement, the short-term, minute-to-minute price chart clearly reflected this information. The stock's on-balance volume revealed forces at work behind the scenes and allowed us to latch on to the institutional money flow, an elephant we rode all the way up to a 100 percent gain. I urge you to take this lesson to heart and acknowledge the distinct advantages this sort of volume analysis offers you as an individual investor.

Returning to my permission-to-buy sector analysis, I identify the strongest industry group within the strongest sector, from which I then generate a list of the most attractive equities and highest-probability candidates. Top-performing exchange-traded funds (ETFs) and mutual funds are added to this candidate list as well. These allow me to appropriately diversify my investments, temporarily park cash in broader market indexes, or fulfill my methodology allocation needs.

Now, most investment articles and books discuss asset allocation. I take this a step further in my own portfolio, using a strategy I call *methodology allocation*. As I have previously described, my methodology is to buy into strength. Even so, I acknowledge the benefits of, for example, buying value or low-beta funds (beta being a measure of a portfolio's volatility relative to the market). With this in mind, I allocate a percentage of my assets to funds that buy value stocks, such as the Sequoia Fund (SEQUX), or very-low-beta funds, such as the Merger Fund (MERFX), which focuses on mergers and acquisitions. I have neither the time nor the passion to appropriately research, analyze, and trade using these strategies because my focus lies elsewhere in the market. I therefore invest a percentage of my assets in funds managed by professionals who do have the appropriate expertise and track record. This allows me to reap the benefits of their investment styles without suffering the time burden myself. I refer to this manner of optimizing my investments within each asset class as niche dominance.

In my portfolio, each of my chosen asset classes is covered by either a top mutual fund with a proven record of market outperformance or a carefully selected ETF with low expenses and a large asset base. Niche dominance is achieved by comparing the best mutual fund in a particular asset class to the best ETF in that same group and then investing in the strongest performing option of those two. If the mutual fund's alpha or outperformance of the market justifies its higher fees over the ETF, then I am comfortable investing in that fund. If not, I save some cash and invest in the more cost-efficient ETF. As a result of this method, I ensure that my portfolio is well diversified across multiple asset classes and that the capital allocated to each class has been invested in the most prudent, strongest-performing option available.

At this point, I look more closely at those high-probability buys—whether equities, mutual funds, or ETFs—and systematically dig in, comparing costs, historical distribution dates, upcoming earnings announcement dates, and historical seasonality trends. As we discussed in Stage 6, buying into a security without reviewing these critical points is careless and potentially suicidal. Keep your profits in your pocket by avoiding high fees, harmful distributions or earnings announcement dates, and historically poor seasonal timing.

■ BATTLE V Methodology

My next touchstone in evaluating a potential buy is to look at how well the candidate stacks up against what I call BATTLE V. This acronym represents exactly the characteristics I look for in determining the attractiveness of a buy candidate, with each letter indicating a key question I ask myself. Together, they form a consistent means of assessing the true, unbiased strength of an equity. Historically, stocks for which I answer yes to all seven questions are statistically more likely to turn into long-term successes and profitable trades. Those questions are as follows:

B Breakout in price

Has the price broken out into new-high territory?

A Accumulation

Is the stock showing significant accumulation?

T Technicals

Are my technical indicators confirming a buy?

T Trend

Is the trend positive in the market, sector, and industry?

L Leadership

Does the stock show strong relative strength and lead its peers?

E Earnings per share

Is it growing and strong versus its peers? When is it due?

V Volume

Does its trading volume indicate demand and institutional sponsorship?

If a buy candidate passes these tests, I begin to explore how it would fit within the boundaries of my trading plan and asset allocation framework. I complete this check from a strategic perspective, asking questions such as, "How much should I buy?" "Which accounts should I buy it for?" and "How does this allocation fit with my present portfolio allocation?" If the stock makes sense according to these strategic parameters, I continue to move forward. Coming closer to actually executing a purchase order naturally brings a heightened sense of excitement and new responsibilities. To control these effects, you must continue to consciously exercise discipline and remain calm.

■ Pyramid Trading

As I discussed in previous stages, I never jump into a position with 100 percent of my intended total allocation. Instead, I use a strategy called *pyramid trading*, in which I carefully ladder into every new position by first buying only a percentage of my desired total investment and letting the market prove me right before I purchase more. This strategy is based in part on the research of trader Ralph Vince. I continue to purchase small, controlled chunks in this manner until I reach my target total investment. In some cases, I achieve only 40 percent of the total investment I initially planned, perhaps because the market stalls or the equity weakens before I acquire a full position.

Pyramid trading is more than a strategy—it is both methodical and statistically sound. Adding to a position in this manner takes advantage of an equity's increasing strength while simultaneously limiting the risk of a fully exposed, 100 percent position in the investment. When as investors we finally make the emotional commitment to buy an equity, human nature tempts us to devour the entire investment in one big bite. In the market, as so often is the case, human nature is simply wrong.

The pyramid method allows you to buy, for example, 25 percent of your intended full position, set your stop, and then wait for the market's next wave to confirm the correctness of your first purchase decision. If the trend pushes higher, the market has reinforced your good judgment and handed you some profit as a reward. If the trend reverses, your stop is executed, your risk is limited, and you book a small loss on only 25 percent of your full intended position rather than a larger loss on its entirety. In general, I pyramid into long positions using a progression that starts with approximately 25 percent of my intended buy, adds 35 percent, and concludes by adding the final 40 percent. I pyramid out of those same positions using a reversed 40–35–25 progression, which reflects the fact that prices tend to fall faster than they rise. In practice, the specific percentages are determined by the state of the market at the time of my trade. I should note that on the buy side I tend to use limit orders for my trades, while on the sell side, urgency may call for the use of market orders instead. This again reflects the impact of the market's gravity on price movements.

In a sense, you must retrain the shopper in you to accept the pyramid trading strategy. Unlike at your local department store, you do not wait for a lower sale price before buying. Rather, pyramid trading dictates the exact opposite. It may seem counterintuitive at first, but you actually want to pay more for each subsequent entry into the market until you have acquired your maximum position. As the equity you have purchased continues to trend up, exercise parallel discipline by moving your stops up to follow the positive trend and protect your hard-earned profits. You can easily take advantage of an equity's uptrend by continuing to add to your profitable positions, controlling your risk as you raise your stops. All of this will prevent a winning trade from slipping through your fingers. Some investors deploy a reverse strategy in which they buy more on subsequent pullbacks. This sort of bottom-fishing at lower prices is, in my eyes, akin to trying to catch a falling knife. Odds are you will grab the blade instead of the handle, painfully slicing your hand in the process.

Six Factors to Determine Your Pyramid Buy-In Percentages
1. The present strength of the overall market
2. The behavior of the sector to which the equity belongs
3. The equity's present market action (price spreads, money flow, trend, etc.)
4. The reinforcing behavior of the equity's sister stocks
5. Other trading activity currently in your portfolio
6. Your own present frame of mind

A primary benefit of pyramid trading comes in its preventative power. It forbids you to add a second position unless you already show a profit on the first. This is a simple, yet strikingly powerful concept you must mentally chisel into stone. In the excitement and madness of a market media blitz, when the hype says one thing but the charts say another, this rule has saved me time and time again. By providing a statistically stronger entry and exit strategy than simply piling into or out of a position, pyramid trading is a discipline that has continually reduced my risk and locked in profits throughout my career in the market.

▪ The Language of the Market

The mechanics of the actual buy involve reviewing daily bid-ask spreads and seasonality data, using minute-to-minute chart data to see specific trading action, and considering both time-of-day and day-of-the-week factors. Multiple computer monitors and live data are essential for improving my timing and the effectiveness of my execution. It is at this point that I really dial into the market and my pending trade. I have found that creating short fact sheets for this part of the buy is a helpful and efficient way to organize my portfolio information. These brief reference lists help me keep track of key information such as my account usernames, passwords, specific order entry instructions, and amounts I plan to use when buying.

Early on in Stage 1, we discussed the importance of learning the language of the market, and now is when this understanding truly comes into play. Today's market offers numerous order options on both the buy and sell sides of every trade. You must learn the differences between, for example, a market order and a limit order. Market makers prefer that you use market orders for everything, but limit orders are often the more appropriate choice. Although learning this language is not a particularly complicated process, it is certainly a necessary one. Carefully read over and memorize Table 7.1, which defines a few of the critical terms you must learn before you begin trading. This list is not exhaustive, however, and it is to your benefit to continue your research to

TABLE 7.1	Order Language Reference Guide
Term	**Definition**
Market order	An order to buy or sell immediately at the best available price
Limit order	An order to buy or sell a set number of shares at a specified price or better
Fill or kill	An instruction to execute a transaction immediately and completely or not at all
All or none	An instruction to fill the order completely or not at all
Stop order	An order to buy or sell a security when it surpasses a specific price
Stop-limit order	Executed at a specified price or better after a given stop price is reached
Not-held order	Gives the broker discretion with regard to time and price to get the best possible price
Day order	An order that automatically expires if not executed on the day it is placed
GTC order	An order that is active until the investor decides to cancel it or the trade is fulfilled

make sure you understand any and all of the market terminology you come across before you push ahead with your investing. Your brokerage house will have helpful resources in this area as well.

■ Buy Routines

Market wizards will tell you that a significant portion of their mastery results from the understanding and implementation of their personal, written money management rules. This is the point in the process when I coordinate my buying plans with my own money management rules, among them, my commitment to creating a start-to-finish investment plan for every trade I make. This helps me think through all phases of the investment. As most investment professionals and experienced traders will tell you, they want to know exactly where their exit is and how they will make sure they do not miss it before they pull the trigger on the buy side.

I formulate both bullish (uptrending market) and bearish (downtrending market) scenarios for the equity I am interested in *before* I trade so that I am emotionally prepared for whichever scenario the market serves up. I determine my stops and enter them before I execute my buy order, either on my own matrix (a soft stop) or on the brokerage site (a hard stop). I then enter triggers and alerts that are sent to me directly from the brokerage. By visualizing the total trade process from beginning to end, both bullish and bearish, I am better prepared for whatever the market has in store for me. This directly translates to more decisive, stress-free trading and greater profits at the end of the day.

With my analysis complete, my routines in place, and my allocations in order, I am almost there. Now I remind myself to remain calm and steady as I prepare to pull the trigger on purchasing a new position or adding to an existing one. When signs appear most advantageous, I am free to execute the buy. Price remains a primary driver, but truly strong, promising investment opportunities will offer greater gains than a few cents, so I do not sweat the pennies when timing my trade.

Instead, I focus on choosing the most appropriate market hours during which to trade the equity in play, a very important part of the buying process. According to historical averages, 33 percent of all trading volume occurs in the first 90 minutes of a trading day, and 21 percent occurs in the last hour. This means that 54 percent of all trading volume occurs during the day's just 2.5 hours of the total 6.5-hour trading day. This can vary due to the liquidity and specific personality of a security, but it is imperative that you carefully choose when exactly you will execute your trade. I suggest charting minute-to-minute data, because it is a helpful way to understand volume movements and determine the most appropriate time of day to trade the equity in question.

A quick side note here about brokerage houses: With multiple accounts across multiple institutions, I know firsthand that not all brokerages are created equal. I personally maintain a relationship with four different brokerages. Throughout years of trading with different brokers, I have found that each brokerage house has certain strengths and weaknesses, often depending on the type of asset you are buying or selling. Because I hold a wide assortment of asset classes in my portfolio, I have my brokerage preferences for each type of investment. Three of the brokerages I use have physical offices near my office in the city, which occasionally provides some important benefits. Overall, while it may require some patience for trial and error, I encourage you to develop your own preferences by experimenting with multiple brokerages. In addition, search for the American Association of Individual Investors (AAII) brokerage ratings, and limit your choices to its top six. Opening accounts with multiple brokerages is a prudent move that will ensure you find the institution that best fits your investing needs.

Back to buying: Just before I pull the trigger, I sit down to review my last-moment, prebuy checklist. For most traders, this becomes second nature—effortless and intuitive with time. It is a simple way of making sure you have covered all your bases before the gun goes off. I speed through one final review and apply my stalking filters one last time. After checking the bid-ask spreads and trading volumes again, I take a deep breath, enter my trade, and send off a new buy order.

As soon as the markets close, I deploy my sisters strategy and assemble a ChartList to monitor the new position I have just purchased. This list includes a collection of charts of not only the equity itself and its industry group but also its sector and a select handful of similar sister stocks I have also chosen to monitor. As I analyze the equities in this ChartList over time, I assess their individual performance as well as the performance of my new purchase relative to its sector, industry, and sister family members. I also monitor the performance of each of the sister stocks relative to industry group and sector. With modern charting technology, this process is much quicker and simpler than it sounds. Most important, it provides an in-depth picture of the exact health of the family of equities, which increases the probability of my primary trade coming out a winner.

The bottom line is that while impulsive behavior may be tolerated at car auctions, it has no place in your investing. It is not easy to remain disciplined and apply these routines, strategies, and methodologies to your investing, but the solid foundation you have built over the previous six stages should empower you as a controlled investor and endow you with an increased probability of making money in the market.

■ Considering Alternatives

Numerous times I have intended to buy a new position, but after familiarizing myself with an equity's sister stocks, I discovered an even better investment opportunity. This happens for a host of reasons, from relative strength to bid-ask spreads to dividend yields. What is important is that I am open to a change of direction all the way through the buying process.

Appealing alternatives present themselves if your methodology incorporates the sisters strategy, whether you are looking at individual stocks, ETFs, or mutual funds. Using comparison tools available on Morningstar.com or your brokerage's website, you can contrast expenses, trading volumes, bid-ask spreads, distributions, and more. Finding a fund with lower expenses or a stock with higher dividends, for example, can help ensure that you are buying into the position most appropriate for your investment objectives. It is just another unique benefit of embracing the sisters strategy.

■ Perfection Paralysis

Too often, new investors are reluctant to trade because they erroneously believe that every puzzle piece of their intensely complex methodology must be in place before they can begin to act. They are paralyzed by inaction, frozen in place by the misguided need to do everything perfectly or not at all. While this may be a commendable objective in many other vocations—open-heart surgery, for example—it is virtually unachievable in the investment arena. A more reasonable approach is to commit to making the most informed decision you can at every moment in time. Use the tools and methodology you have at hand, knowing full well that you will go back and make changes and improvements along the way. This will move you in the right direction as an investor and toward what amounts to an acceptable personal definition of perfection—one you can live with.

We traders must be content with eagerly seeking the promise of perfection while knowing in the back of our minds that—like that greyhound at the racetrack—we will never actually catch the rabbit. Remind yourself after each trade that you are a *recovering* perfectionist. If you are willing to live in the middle space between perfection and failure and you can embrace the gray area that is the stock market, you will succeed as an investor and profit handsomely in the long run.

As a buyer in the stock market, the key to your success is to constantly stare into the mirror and reflect on your investing actions with brutal honesty. Commit to both identifying and improving upon the weaknesses of your investor self, while commending your strengths as well. Address your personal trader's tics—the small things here and there that keep you from performing at your best. Confront your fears and overcome your desire to strive for perfection in every trade. Your trading journal will become your very best friend here. Investing requires unique mental faculties and the ability to follow strict rules about what you will and will not do, but beyond these rules, there will always be some degree of the uncontrollable or the unpredictable. We are, after all, human.

If you look under the hood of extraordinary traders' practices, you will find without exception that there are two critical components in their success. First, they have put in place effective money management rules, and second, they possess the emotional equilibrium to follow those rules without fail, even when the market tries to distract them and break their discipline. Overall, you must accept the uncertainties that come with the stock market. Wholeheartedly buying into the laws of probability is imperative in this regard. It is simply impossible to win 100 percent of the time. Even so, the fact remains that, through diligent and directed effort, you can shift the probabilities in your favor. Learn to accept probabilities for what they offer you, not fight them for what they do not. Control what you can, and don't waste precious energy worrying about what you cannot. Only then will you truly be free to grow and prosper as an investor.

■ Commission-Free Mind-Set

Allow me to let you in on a little secret of mine: I do not pay a dime in trading commissions to my brokerage. Okay, that is not exactly true. I pay the $5 to $10 fees just like the rest of you. The difference, however, is that I have chosen to completely ignore commission costs in my investing, adopting a free-trading mind-set that boosts my willingness to act.

The act of buying a new position is a complex exercise because so many complicated emotions, events, and signals can influence your actions. Yes, tax consequences matter, and allocation decisions are also important, but what is most required at the buy stage is decisiveness and a firm response. Anything and everything that might stand in the way of that—regardless of the size of the speed bump—you must purge and completely banish from your trading psyche. Worrying about commission costs or factoring them into your investing equations will only hurt you. If you can emotionally embrace the mantra that trading is free, you are more likely to do what the market is telling you and accomplish exactly what you need to do. Being even slightly anxious about a trading commission might cause you to pause just enough for the market to move against you far more than the cost of the commission.

■ Invest Like You Drive

For as long as I can remember, one of my closest personal friends, Dan, has worked as a prison chaplain in Oregon. After every visit, I walk away with wild stories of his experiences at the jail, with unique insights only Dan can provide. Some time ago, one of these tales led me to draw a strange yet interesting parallel between prisoners and investors.

Dan observed that some of the first-time prisoners he sees are people who have made poor decisions, end up in jail, and are subsequently scared straight. They learn from their mistakes and do not make bad choices again. The repeat offenders, however, are people who continually make bad decisions without ever learning from their mistakes. It is as if they are driving down the highway of life looking only at the car directly in front of them. They see each decision and event in life as an independent, stand-alone occurrence when, in fact, all decisions inevitably have greater ramifications and connections down the road.

We can again think of this in terms of drivers on the highway. Most reasonable drivers are looking four to five cars ahead. That way, if a problem occurs suddenly, the red brake lights of car number five provide an early warning signal that indicates a potential roadblock or stoppage is ahead. This gives these drivers time to act appropriately and avoid a collision. The repeat offenders in the prison system are unable to grasp the consequences of today's actions because they are not looking ahead to car number five. Instead, they stare only at the car directly ahead.

I have witnessed exactly the same behavior among impulsive investors who fail to pay attention to car number five and instead focus only on the taillights directly in front of them. Successful investors, however, are looking much further down the road. As they consider buying into a new position, they ask themselves questions such as:

1. How does this trade fit with my investing goals?
2. Does this position follow my trading rules?
3. Does this trade allow me to execute my methodology as it was intended?
4. If this is my first position, how will I ladder into subsequent positions?
5. What is my exit strategy? Where will I place my stop?
6. Is the reward-to-risk ratio on this trade acceptable for me?

As you drive down the highway of the stock market, keep your eyes ahead of you, and don't fixate on only the car immediately in front of you. All your actions have ripple effects and consequences, and you must be constantly on the lookout for warning signs of changes to come and problems that may arise. Repeat-offender investors simply buy equities and fail to consider the consequences those actions will carry down the road. My suggestion: Invest like you drive!

■ It's All about Stress Control

I have so far encouraged you to maintain a calm and collected mind-set, focusing on execution rather than immediate outcomes, throughout the buying process. Over time, this will lead to greater profits, but it is not an easy task, and it requires total emotional control. You must keep your balance, rhythm, and patience. As I have said before, the markets are always coming up with ingenious techniques to make you lose your cool, make you frustrated or mad, or bait you into doing the wrong thing at the wrong time, even when deep down you know better. Successful investors do not allow the markets to affect them in this way.

Just like a great painting, all good trades begin with a blank canvas. Winning traders first paint the trade in their mind's eye so that their emotional selves can reproduce it accurately, with clarity and consistency, free from emotions as the markets play out. The here and now is all that matters. You cannot think about the last trade that could have, should have, or would have been. Instead, you must erase your previous emotions, remaining utterly unfazed by what has come before.

Whether you are playing a round of golf or trading the stock market, optimizing your performance is all about stress control. I met with a talented money manager for lunch many years ago, and I was struck by a small insight he provided into the strength of his emotional resolve: He claimed that if you were sitting across the table from him after both a $10,000 loss and a $10,000 profit, you would be unable to tell the difference based on his outward reactions. This gentleman was so in tune with his emotions and so in control of his responses that neither a significant financial deficit nor a dramatic profit could visibly stir him. Needless to say, I would not want to be a member of his weekly poker gang. I have remembered that conversation all these years and have tried to model my own behaviors after him. As I trade, I imagine an observer sitting across from me. My intent is to leave this fictitious observer with utterly no impression of my results. I work to keep a level head and remain calm under pressure, whether positive or negative. This powerful ability can lead to greater stability in your investing efforts.

I relate this to an article in the *Wall Street Journal* about the research of Dr. Robert Goldberg, who has helped golfers ward off stress-induced fits commonly known as the yips. The golf course can be a treacherous and unforgiving place, where even the best players in the world are susceptible to tortured mental states—often at the most inopportune times. Believe it or not, there have been stories about professional golfers being hospitalized with severe panic attacks. The takeaway here is that trading, just like golf, is as much about the mind as it is about the data. Dr. Goldberg's approach to curing the yips is a wristband that measures stress in real time by shooting small electrical charges into a golfer's sweat glands. The data is then sent to a smartphone via Bluetooth and displayed as a stress graph, with peaks and valleys showing the degree of discomposure experienced by the golfer. Dr. Goldberg's research has found that the more accomplished the golfer, the more his or her stress level remains static during a swing and throughout the entire 18-hole round.

It is unfortunate, but this sort of temporary mental breakdown often affects even the market's best traders. The breakthrough, however, is that both golfers and traders can now use information on their stress levels to understand what triggers their stress—on the putting green or in the trading room—and then go about unearthing solutions. If you can recall a specific trade in the past during which you were clearly the architect of your own demise, perhaps Dr. Goldberg's wristband could be of service to you next time. At the very least, it might provide some useful insights into what is holding you back from achieving peak performance.

With a few caveats and some generalizations, Dr. Goldberg's research has found that the more accomplished the golfer, the better his or her ability to moderate stress during play. Likewise, for a trader, even a small amount of stress can cause your heart rate to rise and the butterflies to begin swarming in your stomach. This can have a direct and negative impact on your buying and selling executions. Think of stress as an investor's kryptonite. It disrupts your equilibrium and affects your clarity of thought, and so any action you can take to minimize your investment yips will directly correlate to greater returns and more effective investing.

To conclude, I leave you with this thought: When I reflect on my investing results as documented in my trading journal, I never focus directly on or worry about my profits or losses on individual trades. Instead, I measure the success of my personal investment campaign by how I demonstrated discipline, consistency, and execution. The mystery of it all is that consistent execution results in consistent profits. Time and experience will teach you that a focus on true and total execution of your trading plan will yield profits. A focus on profits themselves will only lead you astray. Once I realized and wholeheartedly embraced this reality, my trading was never the same.

Key Takeaways

- The BATTLE V methodology applies consistent criteria to all potential investment opportunities that can help you find stronger buy candidates.
  - **Breakout:** Has the price broken out into new-high territory?
  - **Accumulation:** Is the stock showing significant accumulation?
  - **Technicals:** Are my technical indicators confirming a buy?
  - **Trend:** Is the trend positive in the market, sector, and industry?
  - **Leadership:** Does the stock show strong relative strength and lead its peers?
  - **Earnings per share:** Is it growing and stronger than its peers? When are earnings due?
  - **Volume:** Does its trading volume indicate demand and institutional sponsorship?
- Use the pyramid buying strategy by accumulating your targeted position in structured percentages rather than buying an entire stake in one trade all at once. This allows the market to give you positive feedback along the way, thereby confirming strong investment decisions and minimizing the cost of potentially unprofitable ones. As always, follow your written trading rules for stocks, ETFs, or mutual funds, and turn to your trading journal for unique insights into what has and has not worked well for you in the past.

Monitoring

Each of us has our own idea of a suitable reward in exchange for our hard work. Returning to my love of all things automotive, which I mentioned in the previous stage, I have been known to reward myself for a major success with something I love—a car—after, say, the sale of a business I started or the closing of a particularly well-executed trade. Your end goals and dream rewards are no doubt different than mine, but I will stay with this car example in order to make my point. Perhaps your dream car is a new Ferrari. You finally achieve your career goals, meet your financial targets, and take delivery of the beautiful red supercar you've always lusted after. You smile from ear to ear when you see it parked in your garage, and rightfully so.

117

But this is not the purpose of such a car. Most owners do not want to simply park it in the garage and let it slowly collect dust. Instead, they want to enjoy the experience of driving a world-class engineering marvel. With that comes the responsibility of using only the proper high-octane fuel, maintaining the fluids and tire pressure, and servicing the car on a regular basis. Without these necessary steps toward preservation, your new dream Ferrari will not perform optimally; instead, it will run just like the old station wagon your parents let you drive as a teenager.

Perhaps you can already see where I am going with this. As an investor, you must maintain your portfolio as you would your new supercar, and this is the process of monitoring. In order to keep your Ferrari running like new or your growing portfolio churning out consistent profits, you must embrace the necessary upkeep routines as an essential part of responsible ownership. Tucked away between the excitement of buying and selling your stocks, it's monitoring that functions as the oil that lubricates your investing engine and keeps it firing on all cylinders.

You Bought It—Now What?

Assembling the essential ingredients of a profitable investing career is no quick, simple recipe, but that's exactly the point. It takes a great deal of study, practice, and work to take an investment from a promising buy candidate through to a cashed-out, profitable trade. Those who can't take the heat, as they say, are best advised to get out of the kitchen.

Consider this: your mind in its untrained state is not a reliable instrument for perceiving the realities of the market because it is too easily prone to emotionality. As a result, it will deceive you. Now combine that natural propensity with the sophisticated Wall Street disinformation machine, which intends to manipulate investors like you to suit its will. The result of these factors is a perfect storm of sorts.

An old trading cliché quips that the quickest way to make a 100 percent return on an investment is to start with 200 percent. There is a great deal of value in this clever little line. Let us say you watch as one of your new positions tears away on a parabolic run, skyrocketing up to 200 percent. At this point, it is not uncommon for greed to take over and fantasies to overwhelm your reason. Hoping that the stock will continue its run all the way up to 250 or 300 percent, you hang on as it turns down and erases half of your hard-earned gain. Too often, investors struggle to remain objective and in control of their emotions. They let their desire for the market to move in the manner they have predicted interfere with their honest analysis of its true actions. As they watch the market begin to fall, they hyperrationalize their actions and convince themselves that the future holds exactly what they envision. In trading the financial markets, you must always remember that you are nothing more than a boat riding the tide, not the tide itself.

Monitoring your investments effectively requires consistent discipline, a focused methodology of routines and tools, predetermined action plans for both bullish and bearish scenarios, and dependable software and hardware. Most important, it requires an unfiltered lens through which you view the market, one that allows you to see it as it really is and not how you would like it to be. The market can indeed be your friend, but you are much better off if you think of it as a police officer with a badge and a gun whose requests need to be taken seriously and acted on in a timely fashion. Together, these create the basis for the following key facets of the total monitoring process, which we will cover in this stage. In many ways, monitoring is a summation of many of the previous stages, combining elements from each to form an effective strategy that allows you to stay on top of your individual investment positions.

■ Revisiting the Investor Self

It is understandable that after the excitement of the hunt (stalking) and the satisfaction of the capture (buying), the process of digestion (monitoring) is not an activity most investors want to dwell on. But don't be fooled: The price of ignoring this crucial activity will lead to issues in your portfolio far more serious than indigestion.

The Achilles' heel for most novice investors is that they are both reluctant and slow to acknowledge the importance of the investor self. As a result, they fail to properly understand the importance of exercising control over the many complicated inner struggles that inevitably arise in the complex equation of successful investing. Stock market mastery can be achieved only when discipline and consistency become part and parcel of an investor's trading personality—particularly today, when financial data circles the globe instantaneously over the Internet. The stock market is no exception to the common saying, "you snooze, you lose," but committed and focused monitoring will keep you wide awake and out of the losers' bracket.

In many senses, monitoring your investments is akin to athletics. At the Olympic level, sprinters' reaction times are measured in hundredths of a second. The quality of their starts coming off the blocks determines to a large degree their ultimate positions at the finish line. Always remember that every other investor's eyes are on the same exit sign you too are staring at. If the trend turns against you, the first loss is always the cheapest. Don't wait for a gift-wrapped invitation to begin selling. The market is happy to continue offering more clues and bearish evidence, but each time it will come at an incremental cost to you. Monitoring is all about you and the investor you want to be—not the investor the rest of the trading world is telling you to be.

Having a system that works productively for your personality and in which you wholeheartedly believe is another essential element of monitoring your investments effectively. The key is to develop a system that ensures you remain engaged in the market and your portfolio's upkeep throughout your trading time frame. This system should take advantage of modern technological powers: the fastest software and the newest hardware. Your system should also put your brokerage house to work for you, requiring you to set alerts and triggers to notify you when items arise that require or deserve your attention. Having portable computer hardware with which you can comfortably travel is the smartest way to remain connected. Thanks to the laptop, the ability to take your office with you has become an indispensable part of any successful investor's monitoring system.

Perhaps even more than ever, the investment-monitoring process requires the implementation of strict, carefully designed routines you can follow within the realities of your other daily responsibilities. Think of this as the ongoing activity module of your investment program. Profitable investors commit themselves to a set of routines and adhere to them with remarkable consistency and dedication. These routines include adjusting stops; anticipating upcoming earnings dates, historical dividends, and distribution dates for stocks, ETFs, and mutual funds; monitoring earnings trends; and watching the market daily—even if only briefly—to remain in the loop and ahead of the curve. Many novice investors dedicate the majority of their time to planting new flowers and a minority to tending their existing garden. Experienced investors, however, are the reverse. They tend to the garden above all else, placing their priority on preserving capital and asset protection. Read that sentence again and truly take its message to heart.

The simple monitoring routines I describe in this stage should provide an outline for you as you craft your own personal maintenance list. Your goal should be to remain vigilant and constantly aware of your portfolio allocations. Never lose sight of how your individual bullish equities are impacting your total portfolio exposure to a specific sector or asset class. A great deal of academic research proves that the construction of a winning asset allocation strategy will determine a significant percentage—most say 80 to 90 percent—of your return at the end of the year.

Another note is that you should archive all your trades. In doing so, you will develop a historical database over time. This will work in tandem with the other sections of your trading journal to provide valuable insights as you reflect back on past winners and losers. Take the time to craft a brief, one-page summary for each trade, keeping notes that detail why you invested in a particular position and the perceived strengths and weaknesses of the equity before you bought it.

Once you have cashed out, revisit your notes to see how you tracked its journey as the trade played out. Review your personal performance to see what lessons you can glean from the experience, and ask yourself what changes you can and should make moving forward. You can achieve significant boosts in the probability of success from the lessons you learn in the monitoring stage, as long as you make the effort to discover and acknowledge them. A noteworthy percentage of your profitability as an investor is determined by how you monitor your kingdom.

■ Market Monitoring

In the monitoring phase, you have a responsibility to follow the market with even more diligence, scrutiny, and attention than you paid during the stalking and buying phases. This is the simple reality of having skin in the game.

You have now placed your money on the line, and your failure to stay on top of your investments could result in an entirely preventable loss. Price movements can be abrupt and unforeseen, and the market will not wait for you. Stay vigilant, and remember that choosing to ignore the markets does not mean that the markets will ignore you.

Your monitoring process starts with a review of your permission-to-buy checklists, which will vary depending on whether the item you are tracking is a stock, ETF, or mutual fund. This process should involve a top-down approach to analysis that begins with the broad market trend and works its way down through the sectors and industries. As during the stalking stage, this increasingly narrower focus will give you a detailed understanding of the current total-market climate in which you are engaged. You can then compare and contrast this climate to the present allocation of your portfolio to judge the probability of its continued performance.

During the buying stage, you aligned your investments with the strongest sectors and industries in an uptrending market. As you monitor the positions you now own, this same idea applies. If you see an equity's industry group or sector weakening, or if you notice that the market trend is shifting, it may be time to rework your allocations, revisit the bearish scenarios you crafted for your portfolio, and consider transitioning your mind-set to one of a seller. These sorts of insights and updated scenarios are a product of a vigilant, committed market monitoring strategy. Keep yourself aware of the general movements of the total market and the appropriate sectors and industries so that your actions remain as current as they were during the initial stalking and buying stages.

■ Adjusting Stops

At this point, let us say you have purchased a new position. You are excited to watch it grow and develop into a winning trade. Playing the part of a wise and rational investor, you set your first stop below the purchase price, at the point that best reflects the risk you are willing to undertake with the position. As the price begins to climb, you elatedly calculate the profits you have earned, proud of your good judgment and well-timed analysis. Feeling confident in the equity's performance, you shrug off adjusting your stop, ignoring this easy task. Another few days go by, and suddenly, the stock price drops aggressively in an unexpected sell-off, washing away half your profit. What you have just experienced is the downside of a failure to adjust your original stop in line with a position's price movements.

Equities in an uptrend move in waves of rallies and reactions. Whether small, intermediate, or large in scale, each upward run is followed by a downward reaction or pullback at some level. For the uptrend to remain in force, an equity's buyers must maintain a majority of control over its sellers. Remember, the stock market is an auction-based marketplace. As an investor, you must acknowledge the time frame in which you have chosen to invest and match it to the price actions of the equity you are trading. An intermediate-term investor should wait for an intermediate reaction, then move his or her stop up to just below the bottom of the pullback. The bottom of a reaction represents a stopping price point, at which point an equity's buyers step in and regain control from its sellers. From here, buying pressures are likely to persist as the equity enters into a bullish trend and prices climb once again. Setting a stop just below this reversal point acknowledges the realistic probabilities of the market and swings them further in your favor.

As an example, refer to the chart of Johnson & Johnson (JNJ) in Figure 8.1. Each time the stock's price achieves a new high, the market is telling us that its buyers are in control. As investors holding this stock, we should return to the area where the buyers first gained control over the sellers and set our stops just below this price. If the battle between the bulls and the bears returns to this same price region and the buyers are unable to wrest control from the sellers, the stops you previously set will prevent this change in the climate from cutting too deeply into your profits. We will cover this again in greater detail in our stage on selling, but the point to understand now is the primary importance of the stop setting and its place within your monitoring routines.

Not adjusting your stops as an equity's price rises is equivalent to buying a shirt and washing it only once. After you first pull off the store tags, you give your new shirt a wash and maybe wear it out to dinner that evening. It fits well and becomes a regular staple of your wardrobe. But along with wearing comes the necessity of washing, for without it the shirt begins to smell and

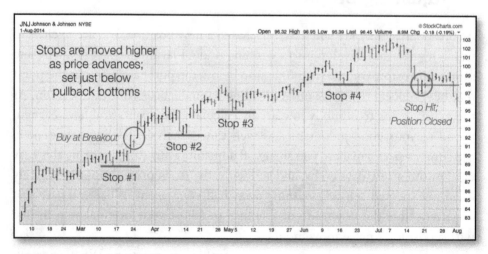

FIGURE 8.1 Adjusting Your Stops
Source: Chart courtesy of StockCharts.com.

the stains set in, becoming permanent. In the stock market as well, this sort of routine maintenance is part of the game. By adjusting your stops, you keep your portfolio fresh, with your profits locked in and looking tidy. I know this habit sounds pedestrian and overemphasized, but I urge you to respect the power that regular stop adjustments offer, because they can quickly become the difference between a slam-dunk, 50 percent return, and a mere 10 percent return. Set your stops just below points of previous support—those price points at which buyers had previously moved in to support the equity and reverse its downtrend. As the bullish trend develops, move your stops upward to trail the positive price changes, setting them just below the reversal points.

How you place your stops should be reflected in the realities of your day-to-day routines. I set and track soft stops on my computer, but I do not actually enter them with my broker. However, I am a full-time investor, and it is my job to monitor the markets closely, keeping a very tight watch over my portfolio. If you have a full-time job and children to raise, then your attention is naturally required elsewhere, and you do not have the time to focus as closely on stop maintenance as I do. In these cases, you have no option but to enter hard stops with your broker. Acknowledging and accepting these realities will only improve the effectiveness of your monitoring system.

No matter how much we wish otherwise, it is a fact: mental stops simply do not work. The best, brightest, and most successful investors I know constantly adjust their stops, alerts, and triggers, either electronically or through a personal matrix of their own design. Most powerful is a combination of hard and soft stops, entered electronically and kept on paper. Remember to factor in earnings dates when you set your stops, tightening them around these announcements in order to combat any surprise downside volatility. Think of stops as a small insurance policy, which can protect your investments even when your mind is elsewhere or your attention is otherwise occupied. Your brokerage house will likely offer electronic alerts as well. Check with your brokerage to make sure you understand exactly which alerts it offers, and determine how you would like to receive them, whether by e-mail, text message, or a notification on your smartphone. These basic routines are a staple of the monitoring process and a necessary element in maximizing profits.

■ Tools, Routines, and Charts

We all know the saying "a picture is worth a thousand words." This is in part why I cannot imagine investing without the aid of price charts, which allow me to ascertain the current position and performance of an equity quickly and efficiently. Almost nothing can hide from the spotlight price charts cast. Where others see simple price lines displayed on just another chart, I see human emotions and all the personal baggage the investing community routinely brings to the table. As I observe individual markets and particular equities of interest, I grow to understand their behavior and learn their specific personalities, if you will.

Jesse Livermore once said, "Every stock is like a human being: it has a personality, a distinctive personality. Aggressive, reserved, hyper, high-strung, volatile, boring, direct, logical, predictable, unpredictable. I often studied stocks like I would study people; after a while their reactions to certain circumstances become more predictable." When there is a change to a chart's normal, expected personality, it sets off my radar and puts me on high alert.

Price charts accurately capture and truthfully quantify the collective psyche of millions upon millions of investors worldwide as the pendulum swings between the extremes of fear and greed. The charts I see are exactly the same as those that you see, with the same vertical lines marking the days' highs and lows and the same histogram below displaying volume. But what makes my charts so effective is that I have watched, read, and traded these pendulum swings enough times to make these otherwise inanimate lines and boxes come alive.

In my mind's eye, I see crowds of wide-eyed buyers and sellers pushing and shoving each other back and forth on the battlefield of prices. The highs and lows for the day represent the scores of the competition taking place between these two parties. Upon the opening bell, a tug-of-war ensues that ends only with the market's close, at which point the day's victor will be crowned. The complexity of this daily battle evolves as the levels of fear and greed fluctuate among participants. Charts offer clear and accurate insights into the true nature of these swings, allowing me to remain objective and make definitive buy and sell decisions on the fly.

As you settle into your new role as an objective market observer, continue to use the charting methods and styles you employed during the stalking and buying stages and the same basket of your essential indicators. By building your own custom charting tool kit, you will develop a consistent level of dynamic proficiency and intuition in your stalking, buying, and monitoring routines. This will increase both your efficiency and productivity, allowing you to maximize the results of your analysis and portfolio-monitoring efforts.

Though your individual preferences will vary, consider the chart in Figure 8.2, which displays my collection of critical monitoring indicators, neatly organized into one easy-to-read format.

Another central component of the monitoring process should be continuing to use the sisters strategy. Because the stock market relies so heavily on groupings, tracking the equities you own as well as their similar sister equities, industry group, and sector provides vital early warnings on the sell side alongside confirmations of continuing strength. As you watch your

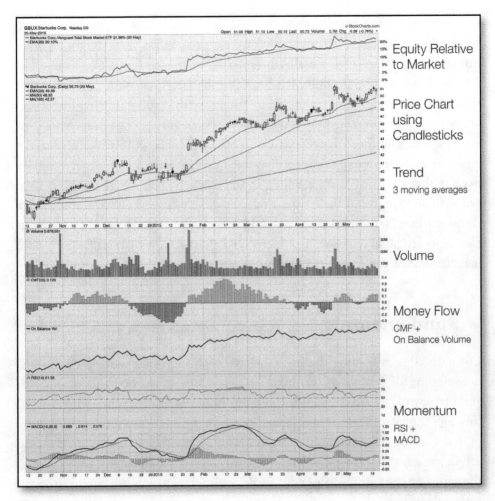

FIGURE 8.2 Monitoring Indicators
Source: Chart courtesy of StockCharts.com.

equity's performance, its sisters will help indicate, for example, that it is an appropriate time to add to a position or that it may be time to take some money off the table and begin pyramiding out.

Ideal here are comparative performance (relative strength) charts, such as those available at StockCharts.com, which make it easy to analyze your equities against their sister stocks, industry group, sector, and the total market. By plotting multiple equities on the same chart, this tool provides a straightforward, yet visually effective method for viewing the strength of your investment relative to the family of other equities associated with it. In addition, continue to use seasonality charts to remain in tune with historical probabilities. And finally, remember that the tracking tools and routines you use must vary depending on the type of equity you are monitoring and its inherent volatility. Hot stocks with a wide trading range must be watched on a daily basis, but an index ETF or a mutual fund can be monitored less frequently. The type of security you choose to buy will determine your routines.

As I have noted before, these indispensable elements of the monitoring stage reflect the analysis tools and routines used in previous stages of your investment process. Don't make the mistake of thinking that their value has declined now that your equity has been purchased. Above all, remember that you now have real money on the table. You carry the risk of it being lost if you are not attentive, making these maintenance procedures in fact more vital than ever before. The most dangerous claim you can make is to classify gains on paper as real. As an experienced investor, I cringe when I hear novice traders declare that they just made a killing in the market, then admit that they have not actually closed out their supposedly profitable trade. You have not made a dime until you sell out of a position and truly lock in your gains. Paper profits can vaporize quickly if you lose focus, and they do not materialize into cold hard cash until you formally close out your trade.

■ Fundamentals

Over decades of trading the financial markets, I have developed a keen understanding of how history repeats itself. I have absorbed the economics and history of the Roaring Twenties from hours of reading and study. I lived through the late 1980s, when Japan was thought to be the unstoppable new global economic powerhouse. I experienced the boom cycle of the late 1990s, when the tech and telecom revolutions had supposedly transformed the rules of economics to permit rapid and permanently sustained growth. One of my key takeaways from these experiences and others like them is that fundamentals do not matter during an emotional crisis. The charts, however, have stayed true, and they have not misled me, despite all the disinformation in the media.

Though I consider myself a technical analyst, I do not want to leave you with the impression that I do not maintain a foot over the line in the fundamentalist camp. It is simply smart business to reserve a place for fundamentals within your monitoring playbook, for the combination of technical and fundamental analysis yields superior investment results. Together, the two form the discipline that I refer to as *rational analysis.*

Because I believe the markets are driven by earnings, my monitoring checklist includes a number of earnings-derived fundamentals, including earnings per share (EPS) and price-earnings (P/E) and price-earnings-to-growth ratios (PEG). Alongside these statistics, I closely follow earnings dates and examine the trends of past earnings data. I also consider analyst reports, monitoring not the projections themselves but instead the trend of their opinions to see whether their projections are increasing or decreasing. Changes here are a catalyst for me to investigate the activity further and with more targeted scrutiny.

As a distant second tier of fundamentals in my checklist, I monitor the news from reputable sources such as *Investor's Business Daily,* Bloomberg, and MarketWatch, if time allows. Finally, I consider the ratings and opinions from the research services provided by my brokerage and from the other resources we discussed during the buying stage, websites such as Morningstar.com for ETFs and mutual funds, and TheStreet for individual stocks. These three tiers of fundamentals-focused routines, fused with my technical analysis routines, form an immensely powerful, rational analysis monitoring system.

■ Allocation Updates

In monitoring your portfolio, properly respect the fact that the markets are constantly moving, shifting, and rearranging themselves. You must match these changes in your portfolio allocations, which you should adjust to reflect the movements and actions of the market. Additionally, depending on the frequency of your trading, track the percentage of your total portfolio that is allocated between different brokerage houses after you make significant changes.

In my mind, I envision the market as a gigantic plumbing system, with pipes of various diameters and alternating connections installed to accommodate the constant flow of money. Today, individuals can move billions of dollars across borders and around the world with the simple click of a button. In this setting, money flows in the market are not only immense but also incredibly fluid, moving at the speed of light.

The good news for us is that the money moving within this plumbing system is subject to the principles of momentum. When institutions begin pumping large amounts of capital through the larger pipes, it creates a sizable force that does not move quietly and cannot be slowed quickly. When the tide of the market shifts to favor growth stocks over value stocks, for example, or when new waves roll in that prefer small-cap stocks to mid- or large-cap stocks, these money flow changes carry tremendous power. Their volume can induce vast shifts in the overall market climate, and the inertia behind them means they can run for long periods of time.

By looking at the larger money flows and assessing the broader movements of the market, you as an individual investor can profitably surf its changing tides. For example, Standard & Poor's divides the U.S. stock market into 11 separate sectors. By looking at money flow and using comparative performance analysis to determine the sector with the greatest relative strength, you can invest in tandem with the market's larger movements by trading sector-wide ETFs, as shown in Table 8.1.

TABLE 8.1	ETFs by Sector
Sector	**Symbol**
Materials	XLB
Energy	XLE
Financials	XLF
Financial Services	XLFS
Real Estate	XLRE
Industrials	XLI
Technology	XLK
Consumer Staples	XLP
Utilities	XLU
Health Care	XLV
Consumer Discretionary	XLY

As your time frame tightens and your risk tolerance widens, you can transition from trading these overarching sectors to trading their underlying industry groups. The health care sector, for example, can be further divided into five industry groups: biotechnology, medical equipment, health care providers, medical suppliers, and pharmaceuticals. If the health care sector is outperforming the rest of the market and biotechnology is the strongest of these five industry groups, you can again invest in an ETF that tracks the biotech industry and reduce your volatility instead of digging deeper and buying an individual stock within what has historically been a volatile industry group.

I submit to you that significant investment returns can be garnered by trading the market's broader movements without ever buying individual stocks. In addition, doing so can also increase diversification and provide more stability to your portfolio, serving as a hedge against the greater volatility that often befalls certain individual stocks.

On a different, yet important note, use your monitoring routines as a reminder to stay up to date with your record keeping, as we discussed in the money management stage. Disorganization and procrastination will cost you in many ways in the market, from increased taxes to poor trade executions. Quicken or other similar software programs will work for you only when you work for them by keeping your data current and accurate.

Finally, I feel that this is an appropriate time to revisit a point I made many stages ago. Remember that there are only two losses a person can experience: loss of capital and loss of opportunity. If we protect the capital, there will always be another opportunity. Without capital, however, there can be no investment; thus, all opportunities become nothing more than painful fantasies. Consider this simple thought: it is better to be sitting in cash and wishing you had a position in a hot stock than having a position in a cold stock and wishing you were in cash.

■ What Is Your Motivation?

Warren Buffett once said, "The stock market has a very efficient way of transferring wealth from the inattentive to the attentive." From what I have seen among thousands of investors in my classes, this committed vigilance is possibly the number one reason institutional money managers outperform individual investors. Money managers do not underestimate the power of disciplined focus, and they have personal motivation to match. Investment firms rely on performance; therefore, managers must follow the program and produce results or risk losing their jobs. To me, this sounds like an immensely powerful incentive. As an individual investor, what can you find in your investing psyche that motivates you in an equally powerful fashion?

It may seem counterintuitive, but successful investing is not really about brains or your IQ. Many brilliant minds who venture into the world of investing know exactly what they need to do, but, unfortunately, they lack the ongoing, consistent discipline to focus on their positions throughout the entire investing process, from stalking to buying and monitoring to selling. These individuals fail to embrace the fact that owning and monitoring equities is a Sisyphean task. Having lived in San Francisco, I am reminded of an interesting fact I once learned regarding the Golden Gate Bridge: This world icon is so enormous that the job of repainting it never ends. By the time the maintenance crew finishes painting the bridge at the north end, the paint at the south end has faded and worn and is in need of another coat. In the fog of San Francisco, rust never sleeps. Your investments operate under a similar reality, and they require the exact same constant maintenance.

I leave you with this: Do what you must to discipline yourself into watching your positions with hawkeyed care. With properly structured routines and the drive to maintain them, you can often accomplish this with just 15 to 20 minutes per day. Understand that the future belongs to those who clearly see the present. When you align your perceptions with the realities of the market, profitability follows naturally. Believe what is happening, not what you think *should* be happening. And finally, rid yourself of any tendencies toward procrastination, and take pride in being an action-oriented investor. In today's market more than ever, action is a requirement, not a choice. With both physical and emotional capital invested in the market, it is your distinct responsibility to remain watchful and attentive.

- Monitoring your investments effectively requires consistent discipline, structured routines, dependable software and hardware, and predetermined action plans for bullish and bearish scenarios.
- Successful investors put their expectations, hopes, and emotions aside to focus on determining the realities of what is actually happening in the markets. Implementing the concept of the investor self that you developed in Stage 3, the monitoring stage requires you to take control of any psychological deficiencies involved in trading. This includes keeping track of every trade—why you took a particular position, what strengths and weaknesses you identified in each security, and how it turned out—all written out in your trading journal.
- Adjust your stops regularly and keep your triggers and alerts up to date. Above all else, stay organized and committed to your investment plan. The monitoring stage is not a time to turn your back to the markets and let your attention falter. It is a time to ramp up your concentration and diligently watch over your portfolio.

Selling

Perhaps you are familiar with the story of the boiling frog. As legend has it, scientists discovered that if you put a live frog in a pan of cold water and slowly apply heat, the frog will not budge. Even after the water reaches a boiling point, the frog will remain in the pan until it dies. Curiously, the frog does not react, because each change in temperature is so slight that it simply continues to adjust to the water as the heat is applied. The frog never realizes that the net result of these temperature changes should be cause for an abrupt, energetic shift in its behavior—a new approach to new conditions. Throughout my career, I have witnessed countless investors suffer from the same tendency toward inaction. They are boiled alive financially as they fail to react to a series of small market changes occurring over time. Collectively, these small changes amount to a major price movement, but without a forward-thinking perspective and a willingness to act, these investors remain in the pan while the heat continues to rise.

An essential part of your role as an investor is to decipher the signals the market provides you and to use them to make informed and timely decisions. Don't be fooled into thinking that the decision to do nothing is a safe strategy: Following the path of the boiling frog by taking no action *is* a decision. For each additional signal the market sends you, it extracts an ever-increasing price. Information will indeed cost you—after all, there is no free lunch in the investing world—and procrastination will only worsen the blow.

Perhaps this is obvious, but I hate to lose. I work very hard *not* to lose. As much as I have tried, I have never grown accustomed to or gracefully accepted my losses. The closest I have come is learning to cope with my losses in a manner that produces the least amount of lingering collateral damage. Bad trades happen. They are simply part of the probabilities. I learn what I can from them and then move on.

In my eyes, there are two types of investing losses you can experience. The first is simply a result of the laws of probability, and it is to be expected even when you flawlessly execute your methodology. When I tell my students that approximately 4 out of 10 trades I make are losers, the novice investors react negatively and begin to question my credibility. The experienced investors, however, nod their heads in supportive approval. These investors understand the probabilities of investing in the financial markets. More important, they understand that what truly matters is not the ratio of winners to losers itself but rather the different ways in which I handle the losing and winning trades.

When I have a loser, I cut my losses quickly to minimize the cost and negative emotional impact. When I have a winner, I let it run, diligently moving my stops upward to protect my profits. As a rule, I never allow myself to give back more than 50 percent of my profit; I always close out a position before reaching this point. Overall, my system works out to be a significant net positive because in this manner, the winners more than compensate for the losers. To return to our baseball analogy from Stage 6, consider this: How much would a professional baseball team pay me if I hit "only" 6 out of 10 times at bat?

The second type of loss requires much more attention and honest introspection. These are those losses that result from ignoring your trading plan or other bad behaviors, and they are what all investors must work diligently to minimize. There should be no "learning to live with it" in the case of this second type of loss, as there was with the first. Appreciate and understand the difference between these two types, and determine not to let your confidence slip in the instances when you executed your trading plan but still sustained a small loss (that unavoidable first type of loss). Allow yourself to accept the fact that even a great trading system in the hands of a seasoned trader will incur losses along the road. Read that sentence a second time, and take it to heart.

Protect your self-confidence by understanding the past cannot be changed. Remain focused, be proactive, and look ahead so that you are able to approach the next trade with a clear mind and an undisturbed attitude. The challenge here is to implement the crucial lessons you learn from reexamining past trades while simultaneously leaving any lingering emotional baggage behind. Regardless of whether your previous trade was a winner or a loser, it must have no bearing whatsoever on the present.

When a loss is the product of poor behavior, however, the ball game is entirely different. If you have a series of consecutive trading losses based on an inability to follow your methodology, the market is telling you to take a time-out. Stop trading, and explore why you are losing control and letting your focus falter. Many experienced traders say that if you lose more than six percent of your invested capital in any one month, you must stop and reassess. Don't let it paralyze you, but instead turn to your trading journal. Perhaps consider paper trading until you regain your equilibrium and confidence. Virtual stock market programs online can give you the experience of investing without the real-world financial impact. Don't avoid the market, but instead spend some time reflecting on your trading discipline and reviewing the rules in your trading plan. Use this time to unplug and forgive yourself, acknowledging that the experience will fuel your growth as an investor, and recognize that—on occasion—we all become emotional. What matters is whether we understand and avoid these same mistakes the next time.

Trading is a journey. Don't let anxiety tarnish your experience or your profits. As I have mentioned previously, whenever I book a loss, I consider it tuition paid to the University of Wall Street, and I tell myself I am paying for the privilege of learning an important lesson. As long as I provide this tuition fee only once per lesson, the cost is tolerable. After years of trading and teaching, my strongest advice is to focus on the process, not simply the dollars. Even the best traders in the world book losses on a regular basis. If you can learn to manage your emotions consistently, follow a consistent game plan, and commit yourself to it with unbending determination, your performance will take care of itself.

Let me share with you a personal story to reinforce this idea. In my previous life as an entrepreneur, I focused intensely on the business, its products, and its management process, because in each case, that was where my passion lay. My motivation was not only to make money but also to see my work succeed by other metrics. Because my focus was appropriately directed, the dollars seemed to simply materialize. I carried this experience forward with me into investing and have realized exactly the same result as a trader. By focusing on the process and execution of my methodology instead of obsessing over my returns, the money has come naturally.

■ Sell on Technicals, Not Fundamentals

Couple the speed at which news travels the globe today with the immensely sophisticated Wall Street disinformation machine, and it is easy to appreciate why I believe technical analysis is an individual investor's primary defense. While fundamentals are relatively slow moving, price charts immediately absorb new data and combine it with pertinent news and events. This instantly reflects exactly how the current auction market of buyers and sellers is reacting. Your success as an investor hinges on your ability to be nimble and remain focused, responding to changes promptly. You must therefore be capable of quickly and confidently pulling the trigger based on the technical signals you see in your charts, even if some fundamentals are apparently glowing with the opposite message.

Used in concert with charting and strong technical indicators, fundamentals offer advantages on the buy side of an investment—a combination I have previously referred to as *rational analysis*. On the sell side, however, fundamentals do not offer this same strength. Here, only the price action displayed on your charts should determine what you sell and how quickly you do so. Price deterioration means that some sellers have begun to sniff out negative pressures. In time, these negative fundamentals will be widely reported, but it is often after the serious damage has been done.

Your selling methodology must maintain a focus on technical indicators and should forgo the use of fundamentals as a primary determinant of your exit timing. With the extensive universe of people and resources willing to help you navigate enticing investment opportunities, the buy side is like an infinite party. The universe of sellers, on the other hand, is finite, and it is also much more solitary. Here, those same investors become your competition. As I have said before, this is the point at which their eyes are fixed on the same exit sign you are staring at. Don't wait for a gift-wrapped invitation to the sellers' party. Instead, find the seat closest to the door.

The reality of investing is that humans are shockingly poor decision makers, heavily influenced by our own judgments and clouded by feelings. Investors tend to see the stocks in their portfolio and the price charts that represent them as emotional dollars, when really they should view them simply as cold, hard numbers. It is the exposure of their hard-earned capital that makes this so difficult. Technical analysis helps investors tame this emotional tiger and maintain a consistent objectivity from one trade to the next. This consistency is what breeds profits.

I often cross paths with budding investors who seem to have two idealized objectives: they want to impress their family and friends with their financial wisdom, and they want to trade without incurring any losses. These goals are akin to wanting to live without being willing to breathe. Contrast them with the goals of experienced professionals, whose major concern even prior to buying into an equity is to visualize their exit so that they do not get trapped in a suddenly widening loss. I once ate dinner with a powerful mutual fund manager whose fund controlled more than $8 billion. He emphasized to me the four elements of selling that he and his management team relied on:

1. Cut your losses quickly.
2. Minimize your mistakes.
3. Conserve your capital.
4. Ask questions later if your trade went south.

This sort of clear and concise philosophy takes emotions out of investing and makes it instead a game of cold, hard truths. Aim to think and act more like these professionals. The results will follow.

■ The Art of Selling

In its most elemental form, selling is an internal struggle that tests an investor's ability to tame the two wild horses of emotion: inner fear and greed. In *Trading in the Zone*, Mark Douglas writes that an investor must address four types of fear:

1. Losing money
2. Missing an opportunity
3. Leaving money on the table
4. Being wrong

Understanding and acknowledging these four fears is only the first step you as an investor must take before you become eligible to earn your selling badge.

For many reasons, there is a specific art to selling. First and foremost, as investors, each of us has our own unique point at which we cry "uncle"—the level where we throw in the towel and sell an equity following a series of negative behaviors and a slip in price. Each of us has our own personal level of tolerance for risk and uncertainty. You must therefore be brutally honest in determining exactly where your "uncle points" are and exactly how much evidence you need to see before you start to take some money off the table. Operating within the boundaries of your personal tolerances will yield superior long-term results, and if you begin to stray beyond these borders, it is precisely this self-honesty that will steer you back to a profitable course.

For this reason, my number one selling rule has two distinct parts. First, have a dedicated selling system; second, develop this system yourself, designing it and embracing it on your own terms. I will share the specifics of my personal system shortly, but I first want to emphasize the necessity of buying into part one. Remember that the market will offer continuous feedback as an equity deteriorates, but each clue it offers costs you more and more money through lower and lower prices. Your system will depend on the types of clues you deem valid and the number of them it will take to reach your personal "uncle point"—when you will pull the trigger and begin pyramiding out of your position.

A selling system is meant in part to protect you from yourself. Its objective is to enable you to lock in profits or minimize losses, protecting your capital. This leads us to the second part: understanding and overcoming the demons that haunt your execution barriers. Some years ago, I polled my students to identify the most common and recurring selling barriers that affected them. Following are the primary results I gathered. As you read through them, ask yourself, "Do any of these apply to me?" If some do, are you willing to do what it takes to overcome them?

- You fall in love with a security and are unable to part with it as the sell signals start pouring in.

- You watch the individual price ticks and miss the big picture. This is similar to our parable about the boiling frog: tracking the changes on a micro level without acknowledging those at the macro level.

- You develop analysis paralysis and endlessly require one more clue before selling.

- You freeze up and simply cannot bring yourself to pull the trigger, despite an equity's obvious deterioration.

I place my trust in charts knowing that they help tame the wild horses of fear and greed. Charting helps me avoid that dangerous mistake I mentioned previously, forcing me instead to view my equities as cold, hard numbers rather than emotional dollars. With this condition under control, I can rein in my fears and take charge of my emotions.

My own selling system incorporates a series of central rules and triggers designed in accordance with my investor self and my personal risk tolerance levels. They include:

- As a precursor to selling, actively adjust your stops to follow along with the upward price movements of an uptrending equity.

- Never give back more than 50 percent of your profit. You must be closed out of a position well before this sort of slippage occurs. This is nonnegotiable.

- After listening carefully to the market and paying close attention to the signals it offers, dump your losers and let your winners run.

- Pyramid out of positions by selling a specific percentage as more clues arrive.

Until you develop a personalized selling methodology, use basic exit triggers, such as moving-average downturns, to initiate a sell order and protect your profits. One simple yet powerful option I recommend in particular is a common chart-based strategy in which you begin selling after a series of descending peaks. As prices start to fall, downtrending equities often experience small upward rallies that represent buying pressure. If a bullish rally does not have the strength to overcome selling pressures, however, its price high will not surpass previous price peaks. Multiple separate rallies that each fall lower than the previous peak indicate that buyers' strength is waning and that sellers are taking control of an equity. This should signal to you that it is time to close out the position and move on. The chart in Figure 9.1 displays this formation

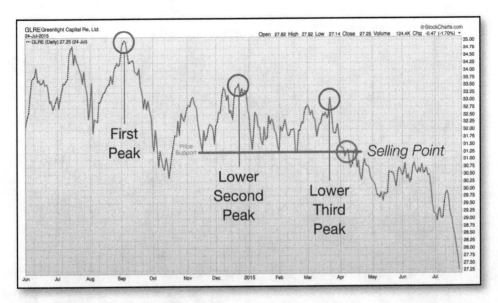

FIGURE 9.1 Three Peaks Selling Strategy
Source: Chart courtesy of StockCharts.com.

in action. As you can see clearly, the three consecutive price peaks are followed by a significant downturn in the stock's price.

The three-peak system's strength lies in both its simplicity and its clarity. It announces to you that, in the ongoing battle between buyers and sellers, the bulls are no longer able to wrest control from the bears. The sellers are now taking charge, and they are preventing the stock from making higher highs. I suggest you practice using the three peaks system by reviewing some of your previous trades to see how it could have applied. Alternatively, you can choose to practice on any listing of stocks making new 52-week lows. From my investment classes, I have learned that investors who practice this exercise by looking at approximately 20 charts become thoroughly convinced of its merits. Once you confirm in your mind the effectiveness of the system, you will be able to better apply it to your own selling.

Another powerful sell-side tool I recommend is the On-Balance Volume (OBV) indicator. In Stage 4, we looked at the accumulation and distribution theories of Richard Wyckoff and discussed how volume analysis can help individual investors recognize the buying and selling campaigns of the big Wall Street gorillas. When a fund or other major institution decides to move out of a position, it cannot simply hit the sell button and instantly drop $100 million of stock back into the market. Instead, these players must orchestrate a careful exit campaign that includes actually buying as well as selling on their way out of a position. By selling and buying repeatedly in very calculated increments to move the stock price horizontally, they attempt to mask their overall distribution campaign.

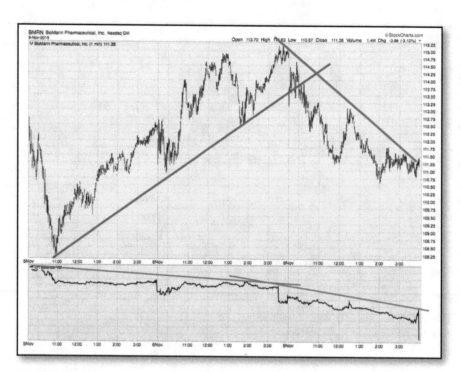

FIGURE 9.2 On-Balance Volume and Minute-to-Minute Data
Source: Chart courtesy of StockCharts.com.

Fortunately, tools such as OBV allow us to identify the negative money flow hidden beneath the surface of these campaigns. The OBV is a simple indicator that maintains a running volume total over a specific period, adding to the total when the stock price closes up and subtracting from the total when the stock price closes down. The cumulative volume additions and subtractions are plotted to form the OBV line. This line can then be compared with the price chart of the underlying security to identify divergences or confirmations. Figure 9.2, for example, shows how OBV on a chart using minute-to-minute data can be used to detect deteriorating support for an equity and recognize potential institutional selling campaigns:

Notice the downward trend of the OBV indicator line as the stock price climbs. Before the price breaks to the downside, the negative trend in the indicator confirms that big volume is on the sell side. As I will describe in greater detail shortly, this deliberate layering on of additional indicators for specific purposes is the basis for my personal selling system.

■ Developing Your Selling System

With practice and experience, your investment system should evolve beyond the three-peaks strategy—but regardless, remember that your selling system must be formulated and in place before you ever buy an equity.

There are many other common selling strategies available for you to learn, use, and modify into a hand-crafted approach you feel comfortable with. Setting an appropriate, historically based profit target is one example that can bring your investing more in line with your unique risk-reward personality and help you choose trading opportunities that make sense for you. It can also provide a very objective, numerical assessment of a position's performance. If this approach appeals to you, the following four methods may also be of particular interest.

1. Set a Target

Within an achievable range, set a fixed price or percentage increase above the point at which you purchased the equity. This should be based on its previous history of breakout rallies and trends. You might set your percentage target for a specific stock at a 15 percent increase, for example, based on its performance in previous cycles.

2. Set a Trading Range

A second option is to use trading-range targets, which apply to any equity moving within a clearly defined trading range. If an equity's price is consistently rising and falling, the pattern quickly establishes levels of support and resistance at the bottom and top, respectively, of each rally and reaction. Support levels indicate points at which buying pressure overwhelms sellers and stops the downtrend. Resistance levels are the opposite, indicating points at which selling pressure overwhelms buyers and stops the uptrend. For equities trading within such a range, investors will buy at former levels of support and set previous levels of resistance as their sell target. Note that a major advantage of this approach is that it can help clearly define ideal points at which to set your stops.

3. Set a Breakout Target

In this third option, when an equity breaks through resistance and out of a well-established trading range, you can measure the height of the prior range and add it to the breakout point in order to establish a potential percentage rally into the next trading range. That area then becomes the sell target. Once again, a pullback into the previous trading range triggers a stop-loss order.

4. Follow the Patterns

Finally, you can use chart patterns for price targeting. Dozens of well-known patterns exist, but two of the most common are the triangle-continuation pattern and the double-bottom reversal. A triangle occurs when the lines connecting previous support and resistance levels begin to narrow over a period of time. If the price breaks above resistance, a conservative target is the previous high before the range began to narrow. A more aggressive target option is to take the length of the entire range at the widest point of the triangle and add it to the breakout point. Next, double-bottom reversal patterns appear as a large W in a price chart, with two roughly equal lows on either side. If the price breaks above the top point of the W, you can set your target price by adding the height of the W to the breakout price. For examples of these two common chart patterns, refer to Figures 9.3 and 9.4.

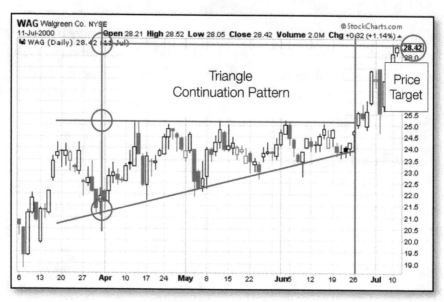

FIGURE 9.3 Triangle Continuation Pattern
Source: Chart courtesy of StockCharts.com.

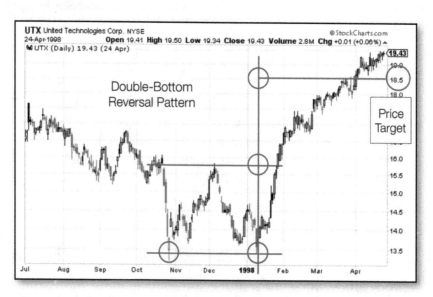

FIGURE 9.4 Double-Bottom Reversal Pattern
Source: Chart courtesy of StockCharts.com.

A Personal Selling Paradigm

As I said before, the four options above are common methods of profit or price targeting. Above all else, their strength is their simplicity and the discipline they encourage.

My own personal selling system, for example, is a bit more complex, so stay with me. It is based on a specific basket of technical clues and a touch of intuition garnered from many years trading the market. My selling paradigm monitors six basic elements: price relative, trend, volume, momentum, bearish patterns, and personal money management rules. I use a simple matrix that expands on each of these individual elements by asking crucial questions that relate to specific indicators from my trading tool kit.

For each question, I check the appropriate answer box—yes or no—with a thick red pen as selling clues present themselves. This hands-on practice pays tribute to the days when technical analysts drew their own price charts by hand. Adding a degree of physical participation to your trading is a powerful way to help you stay honest about the true behavior of your portfolio because it offers clear and undeniable evidence of deterioration. For me, the red pen serves this function. As the sell signals begin to pour in, it becomes increasingly difficult to ignore a vertical column filled with bright red check marks.

Selling is a challenge for us all. It is just human nature. When the market is telling you what you may not want to hear, you must force yourself to listen closely, put your biases aside, and act appropriately. Learn to move from trade to trade without carrying the emotional baggage that accompanies the highs and lows of previous profits and losses. It helps to think in terms of probabilities rather than dollar values. When you take a small loss, tell yourself that you have paid your tuition to the University of Wall Street and are now one step closer to your next big winning trade. After you sell out of a position, try to ignore it for a minimum of two weeks. This will prevent you from second-guessing your actions, which can be toxic.

The six elements of my personal selling paradigm are listed below along with the crucial checklist questions I consider in determining my exit strategy for a position. The charts included for each element also provide some more real-world examples to help you better visualize and apply each one.

A note on chart patterns: I recommend researching some of the most common price chart patterns. I follow a few key patterns, which we'll get into briefly in just a moment, but many others exist as well. One particularly helpful resource for this task is the chart patterns database available for free in the ChartSchool section of StockCharts.com. This extensive resource can also be helpful for other general market education needs, since it includes dozens of detailed articles on all essential technical indicators, charting styles, and analysis techniques.

Again, appreciate that we all have different risk tolerances: I know that I've hit my uncle point when my selling matrix shows about seven red check marks. At that point, I begin to take money off the table by pyramiding out. Your risk tolerance may require more or less evidence. Perhaps it takes 10 or 12 red flags for you to cry uncle. Experience will dictate how many clues you demand from the market before you begin taking money off the table. The critical point here is that I constantly monitor the following six elements, each with its own individual checklist that helps me to track the overall health of an equity. Together, these elements and their respective checklists form the basis of my personal selling paradigm.

Price Relative Price relative measures an equity's performance compared with that of another stock, fund, or market index (Figure 9.5). The following questions can help you more accurately determine a position's performance so you can strengthen your selling plan:

- Has there been a deterioration in the equity's relative strength versus the market?

- Has there been a deterioration in the equity's sector relative to the market?

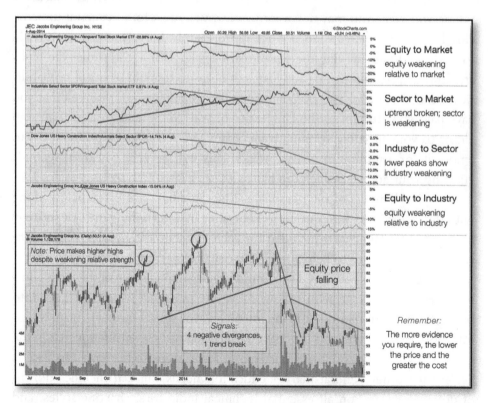

FIGURE 9.5 Price Relative Selling Chart
Source: Chart courtesy of StockCharts.com.

- Has there been a deterioration in the equity's industry group relative to its sector?

- Has there been a deterioration in the equity relative to its industry group?

- Has there been a deterioration in the equity relative to its sister stocks?

Trend Signals Regardless of the time frame, there are only three possible trend phases in which any given security can exist: an uptrend, a downtrend, or a sideways trading range (Figure 9.6). Trend signals occur as equities transition from one phase to another. The following trend-related questions help identify these transitions that prepare you to take the appropriate selling action:

- Have the existing trend lines (long-, intermediate-, and short-term) been broken?

- Have there been negative changes in the slope or direction of the Moving Average lines?

- Have there been Moving Average crossovers?

- Has the equity's price broken the Moving Average support lines?

- Has there been a break in the short-term support and resistance levels? An intermediate-term break? A long-term break?

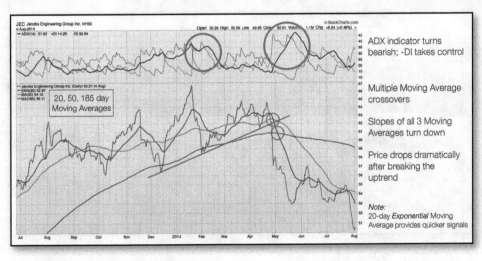

FIGURE 9.6 Trend Signals Selling Chart
Source: Chart courtesy of StockCharts.com.

Volume Volume analysis can provide clues that help reveal the true intentions of the institutional money managers and announce likely price reversals.

Tracking On-Balance Volume and money flows can uncover the campaigns of the big money behind a security as the institutions attempt to mask their larger objectives. Using volume to your advantage is an important component of any robust selling system (Figure 9.7).

- Is on-balance money flow weakening? Is it making lower peaks?

- Is volume fading on upward rallies?

- Is volume increasing on downward pullbacks?

- Is volume increasing at breaks in the trend lines?

- Is volume increasing through previous price supports?

- Is volume increasing at breaks in the moving average lines?

- Have there been any climactic volume or price spikes of particular note?

- Is the daily price range expanding? Has volatility increased?

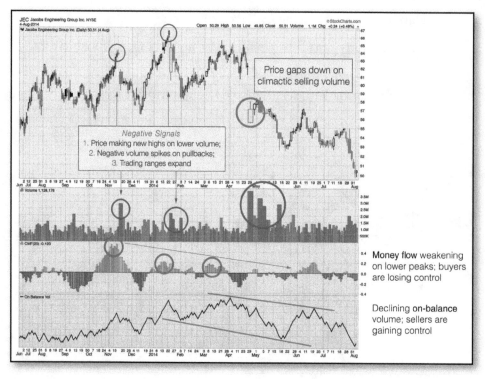

FIGURE 9.7   Volume Selling Chart
Source: Chart courtesy of StockCharts.com.

Momentum   Momentum is a significant concept at play in how prices move in the stock market. Similar to the laws of physics, momentum begins to slow well before a stock's price reaches its peak. Using technical momentum indicators can provide critical early warning signals of pending price tops and upcoming reversals (Figure 9.8).

- Is the Relative Strength Index (RSI) tracing out lower peaks?

- Is the RSI beginning to hover below the midpoint equilibrium value of 50?

- Are rate-of-change peaks confirming or diverging from price peaks?

- Is the Moving Average Convergence Divergence (MACD) indicator acting bearish?

- Are two out of the previous three items giving bearish signals?

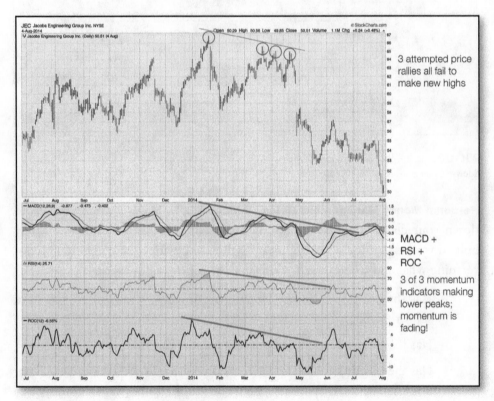

FIGURE 9.8 Momentum Selling Chart
Source: Chart courtesy of StockCharts.com.

Bearish Patterns Price patterns represent human emotions, which have remained surprisingly constant for centuries. Recurring bearish price patterns are worthy of your attention. Learning to recognize common bearish patterns can dramatically improve your selling methodology (Figure 9.9).

- Has the equity experienced a steep parabolic run?

- Has there been a head-and-shoulders topping pattern? (According to Thomas Bulkowski's *Encyclopedia of Chart Patterns*, this is one of the highest-probability topping patterns.)

- Has there been an island-reversal pattern?

- Has there been a triple-top reversal pattern?

- Has there been a double-top reversal pattern?

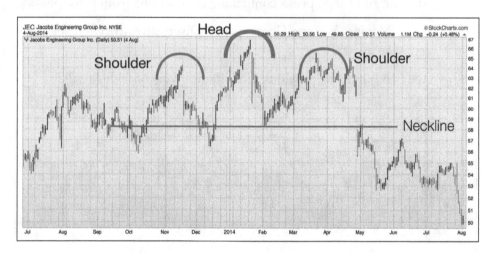

FIGURE 9.9   Bearish Patterns Chart
Source: Chart courtesy of StockCharts.com.

Personal Money Management Rules   Think back to Stage 1 when you wrote down your clearly defined money management rules. In the same way they helped you determine what to buy and when to buy it, they will help you determine what and when to sell. Consider the following questions:

- Has the position hit a predetermined dollar loss maximum you have set for trading?

- Has it hit a predetermined percentage loss maximum?

- Has the position rallied and achieved your profit or price target? If so, don't let yourself become greedy. Be willing to begin pyramiding out and protect your profits.

- Does your portfolio require rebalancing to align with your asset allocation targets?

■ Mutual Fund Sell Signals

Mutual funds present unique challenges on the sell side because they do not offer trading volume clues in the way individual stocks or ETFs do. My backdoor solution to this dilemma is to track the price performance, volume, and money flow of the fund's top 10 largest equities. In general, their actions will have a significant impact on the overall performance of the fund because they account for a large percentage of its assets under management.

Two historical examples of mutual funds that operated in this manner are the Fidelity Select Wireless fund (FWRLX) and the Marsico Focus fund (MFOCX). In October 2014 two equities—Verizon and Qualcomm—accounted for 27 percent of the Fidelity Select Wireless fund's portfolio. At the same time, 20 percent of the Marsico Focus fund's portfolio was in Gilead Sciences, Facebook, and Biogen. As such, the performance of these two funds was highly dependent on those equities that made up such a significant percentage of their portfolios. In situations like these, we as individual investors can monitor the volume and money flow of the funds' primary holdings, gaining what amounts to X-ray vision into the funds' current and expected future performance.

The chart in Figure 9.10 presents a pure technical approach by illustrating four reliable sell signals before an upcoming downturn in a mutual fund—in this case, the Direxion Indexed Commodity Strategy fund (DXCIX). First, as the relative strength indicator starts to slip below 50, momentum fades. The relative strength indicator then tracks out lower peaks, causing a negative,

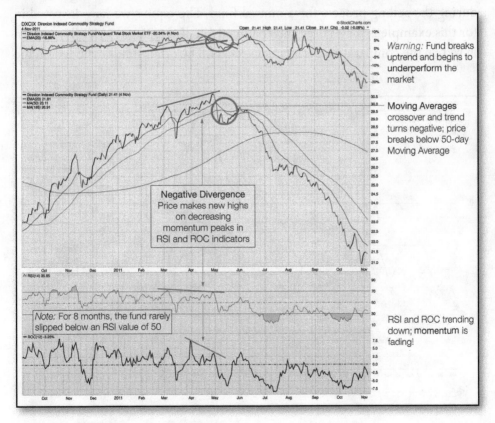

FIGURE 9.10 Mutual Fund Sell Signals
Source: Chart courtesy of StockCharts.com.

bearish divergence with price, which continues to make new highs. The next warning occurs as DXCIX suddenly and severely begins to underperform the market, represented by the Vanguard Total Index (VTI). Finally, capitulation results in moving averages turning downward and negatively crossing, with price also breaking below the 50-day moving average.

Selling with the Sisters

Throughout the stalking, buying, and monitoring stages, we have continually returned to the sisters strategy. Selling is no exception: this same concept also functions as an exceptionally effective selling tool when you gear up to exit out of a position. Just as it can provide early warning signals during previous stages, it does the same now, on the downside. It works regardless of whether you are trading stocks, ETFs, or mutual funds, because the financial markets rely so heavily on groupings. Note that selecting the appropriate sisters is a skill set novice investors will have to nurture. The process is not overly difficult, and experience will result in better picks over time, but take care early on to select the most compatible and appropriate sisters you can.

The chart in Figure 9.11 shows an example of the sisters strategy at work during the selling process for a mutual fund. The equity we have invested in for this example is the Artisan International Small Caps fund (ARTJX), shown in red on the comparative performance chart. The other funds included on the

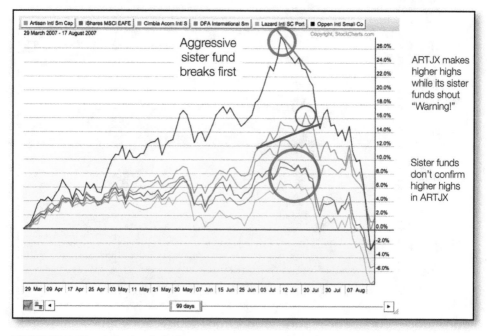

FIGURE 9.11 Selling with the Sisters Strategy
Source: Chart courtesy of StockCharts.com.

chart are the sister funds we have chosen to monitor in addition to the Artisan fund itself. Take note of three pieces of this puzzle: first, the more aggressive sister funds, which rallied the most in the uptrend, are the first of the group to break and enter a downtrend. Shortly after, we see that Artisan itself continues to rise and manages to make new highs, but the weaker sister funds in its family cannot follow suit. They shout "Warning!" and begin to decline—thereby not supporting our equity, Artisan.

After this new high, Artisan finally breaks and joins its sisters in a downtrend. Without our diligent monitoring of our equity's sister funds, Artisan's new high would have misdirected us into a false sense of optimism, followed only by supreme disappointment as the price tumbled. Instead, the sisters strategy provided multiple early warning signs to indicate that it was time to take some money off the table. I encourage you to carefully study the chart above and use it as a reminder of the power that this strategy can offer on the stalking, buying, monitoring, and selling sides of your investing.

◼ Sell-Side Pyramid Trading

As I have mentioned previously, the pyramid structure we used in purchasing our equities also applies to our exit, although somewhat accelerated. Though this approach to closing out a position is tiered in percentages rather than a simple dump-it-all method, it should reflect the fact that the market moves downward approximately three times faster than it moves upward. On the buy side, your entry strategy might use purchase percentages of roughly 25, 30, and 45 percent. Your exit strategy on the sell side should use a structure that is nearly the reverse of your entry percentages—in this case, you might sell in stages of 50, 35, and 15 percent.

Just as on the buying side, the pyramid strategy adds more stability and security to your trading on the way out of a position, letting the market prove you right gradually as you exit instead of jumping out entirely at once. I have occasionally sold half of a position on a pullback only to have the remaining 50 percent double in price. Sound mathematical reasoning and numerous academic studies justify the effectiveness of this approach, and it is to your distinct advantage to put it to work for you.

◼ The Endowment Effect

The academic community has published countless papers proving that investors attach significantly more value to the positions they currently own than to those that they do not. This phenomenon—known as the endowment effect—is one psychologists frequently study. For example, some studies take a set group of participants, such as college students in a particular course, and split them into two groups. The first group is given an inanimate object, such as a coffee mug, while the second group receives nothing. When the students are later asked to assign a dollar value to the coffee mug, those who were given a mug report dramatically higher valuations than those who were not given a mug. Having been endowed with a mug, even for only a few minutes, the subjects take ownership of it and factor that emotion into their determination of its value.

This same effect is at play when you invest in an equity. In years past, I have fallen victim to it as a trader, as have many of my colleagues and students. A long, profitable run from the biotech industry, for example, left me emotionally overvaluing my position; then the industry's strength began to fade, and it started to underperform the market. Even in the face of multiple lower peaks and negative money flow within sister stocks, I struggled to embrace the changing winds. Blinded by profit and distracted by visions of continued rallies, I let my emotional attachment to my existing position step in the way of my rational mind. Although my selling matrix was lighting up with bright red check marks, my commitment to my trading plan slipped.

In the end, procrastination diminished my returns because I grew too fond of my biotech positions. I began to personally filter what the charts were telling me, allowing my own hopes to creep into my interpretations in an unhealthy manner. Standing in the rain hoping for the sunny skies to return, I became greedy and was slow to react appropriately as a result. Let my mistake be a lesson, so that you refrain from making the same blunders yourself. Factoring in your personal capital, time, and energy, investing leaves you highly susceptible to the impact of the endowment effect. If you see yourself forming this sort of emotional attachment, step back, breathe, and do whatever it takes to rediscover your rationale and your sense of objectivity.

■ The Investor's Trail

We as investors are imperfect creatures living in a complex world. We are destined to stumble and fall somewhere along the way. It is simply part of the probability game that is the stock market. One day in the near future, you will probably find yourself among the investing losers, just as surely as any exceptional salesperson will occasionally come across the impossible prospective customer who rebuffs even the most compelling pitch to buy. Take comfort knowing that when you land yourself in this spot, you will not arrive alone.

At the moment of a loss, you have a responsibility to yourself to siphon off the key insights you can take away, then brush off the experience and put the bad trade completely behind you. Every trade offers a lesson, and the losing ones are just part of your education as an investor. Rather than ignoring the markets' teaching moments and hanging your head, keep your eyes on your long-term objectives, and tell yourself exactly what you will do differently the next time around.

Think of bad trades as an opportunity to begin again, a chance to come back and rise to greater heights. You have now ventured out onto the investor's trail, one carved by missteps and built on hard-earned insights. There is no map for this journey, no trail guide for the undisciplined or uncommitted. Although treacherous at times, you must have faith that the next mile marker and fresh welcome sign are waiting to greet you just up the road. With your focus on the trail ahead and your eyes looking toward the future, it is your belief in this path that will lead you to the picturesque scenery at the top of the mountain.

Key Takeaways

- The careful monitoring efforts that you put forth in Stage 8 give you an edge when it comes time to sell. Fundamentals are fine on the buy side, but on the sell side, they are often too late to the party. Only price action should determine what you sell and how quickly you pyramid out of a position. The market and the specific securities you own will give you small clues about how it is changing, and a well-crafted selling system will help bring those clues together to paint a clear picture.
- It is imperative that your selling system be formulated and in place before you buy any position. This sort of preparation will help ensure your success. The six elements at the center of my personal selling paradigm are: price relative, trend signals, volume, momentum, bearish patterns, and the personal money management rules you set in Stage 1. Until you develop a personal selling methodology, use simple triggers such as moving averages or the three lower peaks to initiate a sell order and protect your profits.
- Just as it was used on the buy side and during the monitoring phase, the sisters strategy is a key selling tool. Determining the health of a stock's sector, industry, and sister stocks can help you better judge when a deterioration in your position may be lurking.
- Take the emotional element out of it and cut your losses quickly in order to minimize the negative impact and reallocate your resources to more profitable trades. Remember that for each additional signal the market sends you, it will extract a price. The more information you require, the more it will cost you.

Revisit, Retune, Refine

The only way you get a real education in the market is to invest cash, track your trade, and study your mistakes. . . . The examination of a losing trade is torturous but necessary to ensure that it will not happen again.

—Jesse Livermore

Before you sprint across the finish line with your arms raised in the air to celebrate your trading atop the winners' podium, there is one final piece of the puzzle you must carefully put in place. As we have discussed before, history is often the strongest indicator available to you as an investor. This applies not only to the performance of the market but also to your personal performance. With your trading journal spread open in front of you, your final responsibility—after every trade you make—is one of thorough reflection. This should be untarnished by any emotional baggage and undisturbed by existing biases.

Revisiting your actions after a trade is crucial to your personal growth and development as an investor. This includes an assessment of your performance not only by the numbers but also according to how well you demonstrated emotional control, adhered to your trading plan and methodology, and executed your routines. Investing is a game of ongoing discipline and self-betterment, not simply one of endless profit seeking. As such, your post-trade evaluations must make a holistic judgment of your successes and your failures, analyzing your investor self in addition to your newly reconfigured financials.

I find it best to approach this final stage by thinking of it as a part of your educational foundation. The market is an extraordinary teacher, but to collect its wisdom, you must be a willing student. With each and every trade, ask yourself what you could have improved upon and what you must do in the future to increase your percentage of winning trades. The market will reward this sort of productive self-reflection handsomely.

■ Cleanse and Move Forward

The beauty of investing is that every trade you make presents a fresh opportunity to reevaluate the strength of your trading system. In doing so, you are able to make a careful inventory of all of your past experiences and investing behaviors, then retune the bits and pieces that need adjustment to optimize your investing platform over time. With a generous batch of personal honesty and humility, this post-trade revision is a deep cleansing that restores and reorders your investing efforts for the future. I know firsthand that revisiting poor trades and bad executions is neither an appealing nor particularly pleasant task, but it is one of the crucial building blocks of your growth as an investor.

As you consider the past and analyze your actions, you will identify the mistakes that need correcting and the system components that require greater attention. The end result of this reflective return is a compilation of the good—a sort of greatest hits from your past trades that combine to form a new and improved investor self with which you can move forward. This transition involves two elements: what you consciously leave behind and what you purposefully take with you. Thinking about the review process in terms of these two categories can be helpful in separating the positives you can maintain from the dead weight you must cut.

In putting myself through this exercise for many years, I have found that a major benefit is that it forces me to determine the instances in which my analysis was correct but my execution was off, and vice versa. Revisiting my trades with these details in mind helps me narrow in on exactly where any issues are occurring so I can determine precisely what I need to improve. Further still, I unbundle my execution and look at both halves of the equation: my technical execution and my emotional execution. Dissecting my total investing process into smaller and smaller chunks brings any nonproductive deviations to my attention. This ensures I discover and attend to these issues properly before I make any further trades. The feedback loop this creates will become both a powerful ally and an important source of your improvement as an investor.

The final step of the Tensile Trading process relies on the Four Rs of investing:

1. Reshaping your learning curve
2. Realigning your thinking
3. Reprogramming your discipline
4. Refining your trading skills

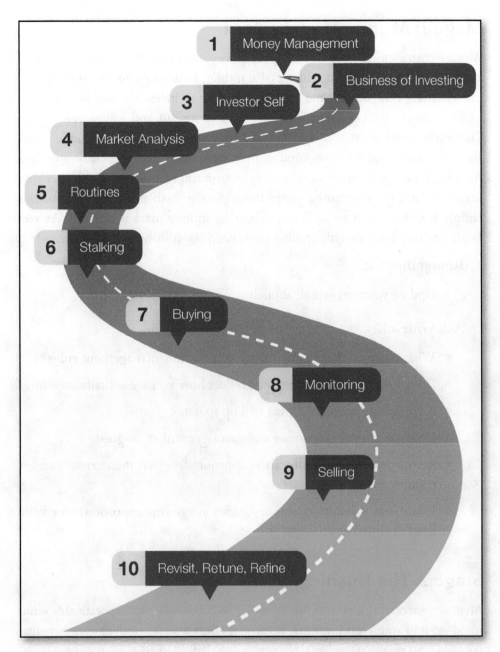

FIGURE 10.1   Revisiting Your Roadmap

With an eye toward these four responsibilities, you can leave behind your old investor self and the imperfections it bore, letting go of detrimental behaviors as you begin your transformation into a new and improved investor self. With this theme of review in mind, let us revisit each of our 10 stages in stock market mastery individually, addressing the checklist items and questions you should consider for each (Figure 10.1).

Stage 1: Money Management

Money management starts with proper organization. It is about acknowledging your true and exact financial standing, knowing your personal goals, and deciding how much time you will allocate to investing. Key here is a set of firm money management rules that you write out and follow religiously. Determine your most appropriate asset allocation strategies, and understand the risks and volatility associated with various asset classes before you dive in. Don't just park your cash in a next-to-nothing percent yield checking account. Easy money can be yours through wise cash management, such as simply transferring it to an interest-bearing money market account. As you begin crafting your specific trading plan, keep the following items in mind:

Remember to:

- Update your net worth annually.

Ask yourself:

- What changed that might impact your money management rules?
- Does your current trading plan reflect how you are actually investing?
- Is your asset protection plan still up to date?
- How can you improve your cash management strategies?
- Is your present asset allocation appropriate given the current market conditions?
- Were your accounting and organization systems appropriate for your level of activity?

Stage 2: The Business of Investing

Mentally, successful investors treat trading as a business. Incorporate this same mind-set into your own investing, because it offers a series of significant benefits. As a starting point, assemble a physical space dedicated to your trading efforts, and invest in the latest and greatest computer system you can afford. Today's market is entirely technology based, and the hardware you use must reflect this fact. Determine the investment time frame most appropriate for you, and remember always that asset protection comes before asset growth. If you protect your capital, there will always be another opportunity. Without capital, however, there can be no investment and therefore no opportunity, either.

Ask yourself:

- Did your information systems, tools, and action plans combine to produce positive outcomes?

- Is your computer system functioning effectively? Is it up to date and secure?

- Are your brokerages servicing your accounts properly?

- Is your tax adviser or financial adviser meeting your needs and expectations?

- Are you comfortable with the office space you have set up for your investing activities?

Stage 3: The Investor Self

Self-honesty is the core of the investor self. Come to know your strengths and weaknesses as an investor—otherwise, the market will extract a painful price for teaching you. Truthfully identify your present level of experience, and learn from other investors' mistakes, using the wisdom of successful traders to your own advantage. Don't underestimate the immense importance of mental discipline and the effect it will have on your success. Most important, commit to keeping a trading journal, either handwritten or electronic. If you are truly candid about your trading experiences, this journal will become your guide to accelerated improvement and consistent profitability.

Remember to:

- Revisit your self-audit with brutal honesty. Expect yourself to change as you grow.

- When you book a loss, you have paid the market tuition to teach you key lessons. Make a list of what you have learned, and take these points to heart. You only want to pay once per lesson.

Ask yourself:

- Have you consistently found a time of day to maintain your trading journal?

- Have any core aspects of your central beliefs changed?

- Have you been keeping up with your reading and personal education?

- How well did you align yourself with the profitable traits of successful market wizards?

- When it comes to the four categories of common investor weaknesses— planning roadblocks, deficiencies in knowledge or education, psychological baggage, and execution barriers—which are holding you back from becoming the very best investor you can be?

Stage 4: Market Analysis

To maximize your probabilities, align uptrends in the general markets with out-performing sectors and industry groups, then determine the best stocks within those industries. These equities will be the highest-probability trades. Use telescope-to-microscope analysis in this stage: Start with the big picture by looking at long-term monthly data, then continue to narrow your focus down to weekly and daily time frames. Your final analysis should use a microscopic lens to zoom in on the minute-to-minute data before you execute any trade.

Throughout this stage, embrace Richard Wyckoff's concept of the composite operator. Monitor volume and money flow to uncover the accumulation and distribution campaigns of large institutions and determine how they impact your own positions. Finally, acknowledge the value of historical seasonality patterns in the market, and appreciate that these recurring monthly trends of strength and weakness across previous years can move the probabilities in your favor.

Ask yourself:

- Is your approach to the market producing consistent profits?

- Does your methodology feel right for you? Were you able to follow your plan?

- Is there another methodology you would perhaps like to try? (If so, try trading with it on paper first.)

- Has your percentage mixture of fundamental and technical analysis shifted?

- Are your present information sources yielding worthwhile results? Should you budget time or money for others? Do you use too many already?

- Have you gained an intimate knowledge of your core set of indicators? Do you believe in them enough to consistently act on their signals?

- How would you rate your improvement as an investor? As a trader? As a market observer?

Stage 5: Routines

Daily, weekly, monthly, and annual routines minimize emotional barriers and impulsive trading while also helping to advance your all-important market intuition. Central among them is your trading journal, which will yield powerful insights and lessons about you and your investing habits when written candidly. Complete your routines first, before you spend precious time reading

Forbes or *BusinessWeek* or watching CNBC. These sources of data provide great entertainment value, but your own trading system must come first. Your routines should reflect the reality of your other commitments. If you can allocate only 15 minutes to investing per day, then your routines must acknowledge that reality.

Daily routines should include reviewing general market trends, trading volume, and momentum. Discipline yourself to monitor all of your open positions; stalk new trades; check your alerts, triggers, and stops each day; and update your trading journal. Weekly routines should include a review of your asset allocations, deeper-level sector and industry analysis, market breadth and sentiment examinations, and intermarket analysis. Distribute these responsibilities throughout the week to ensure that they do not pile up on you suddenly on Friday evening. Your monthly routines should break down annual to-dos into manageable portions during the course of the year, preventing a buildup of panic and stress at year-end.

Remember to:

- Recognize when you begin to distort market information to fit your beliefs. Knowing these trades are those most likely to fail, force yourself to neutralize your feelings, manage your perceptions, and accept whatever realities the market presents.

Ask yourself:

- Regarding the time you have allotted to investing, is it too much? Too little? How is your balance?

- Can you shift some daily routines into weekly routines? Weekly routines into monthly routines?

- Are the observations in your trading journal yielding robust payoffs? If not, why?

- Were you able to spread out your annual to-dos comfortably over the course of the year?

- Are any habits wasting your time, such as watching too much business news or endlessly surfing the Web?

Stage 6: Stalking

Stalking is the disciplined art of methodically knowing where to look, what to look at, and how to look at only the most promising, timely potential investments. To do so, you must limit your sources for ideas and deploy screens that winnow an infinite number of choices down to only a few of the most promising candidates. In the course of stalking, stay committed to your trading plan, and focus on the time frame and security types with which you are most at ease. Review your past winners, and replicate stalking efforts that have been successful for you in the past. Large institutional investors target the best stocks in the hottest industries. Using money-flow data, you can determine exactly which equities they are buying and follow along for the ride. The market will tell you if you should be trading the long-side uptrend or the short-side downtrend. Leave simultaneous long-short trading to the hedge funds.

Ask yourself:

- Have you recently updated your asset allocation profile?

- Do your core-and-explore percentage allocations need to be readjusted?

- From where did your most profitable ideas originate? What about your least profitable?

- Do you have the right number of tools in your kit? Would focusing on fewer elements yield better results?

- Are you costing yourself profits by insisting on using the cheapest broker and only free websites?

- Which do you enjoy most as you invest: stalking, buying, monitoring, or selling?

- Do you have all four in equilibrium? Or are you enamored with one at the cost of the others?

Stage 7: Buying

A significant percentage of a day's trading volume occurs in the first hour (which is dominated primarily by individual investors) and the last hour (which is dominated primarily by institutions). The times between are often volatile, trendless markets with higher bid-ask spreads. Factor this into your time-of-day buying decisions.

Your written trading plan should detail buying rules for each type of equity you trade, whether stocks, exchange-traded funds (ETFs), or mutual funds. Although counterintuitive, research has shown that simple trading strategies consistently outperform more complex models. Employ a detailed, written investment methodology—such as my BATTLE V—so that you apply a consistent set of criteria to potential trades and remain clear minded when deciding between candidates.

Also imperative for this phase is knowing the language of the market. This will contribute significantly to your profitability. Failing to learn the difference between a market order and a limit order or misunderstanding how they are used will wastefully cost you money.

Employ the pyramid strategy, accumulating a target investment in stages rather than buying the entire position in one trade. This allows you to collect feedback from the market, which will help you determine the wisest amount and rate of acquisitions. Letting the market prove you right on your first position before assuming a second reinforces profitable decisions and minimizes the impact of incorrect decisions.

Next, make sure you understand the impact of properly timing your investments. Take into account the distribution dates and tax consequences before you purchase any security.

Ask yourself:

- Did your money management rules serve you well, or do they need to be tweaked? Did you adhere to them?

- Do you feel like experimenting or retesting a previous variation of your methodology?

- How disciplined were you in pyramiding into your positions?

- Does the explore portion of your portfolio have too many positions? Too few?

- If you had to add one new investment rule, what would it be?

Stage 8: Monitoring

Effective monitoring requires consistent discipline, carefully chosen routines and tools, dependable software and hardware, and predetermined action plans for both bullish and bearish scenarios. The tools and routines you use should vary depending on the type of equity you are monitoring and its inherent volatility. A hot stock needs to be watched daily, while an index ETF or mutual fund can be monitored less frequently.

The sisters strategy is a critical element of this stage. Tracking the equities you own as well as their sister equities, industry group, and sector will provide vital early warning signals. Ultimately, stay focused and diligent. You now have real money on the line, so you must remain even more committed than before. Remember, vigilance is the price of profits.

Remember to:

- Review every chart of every position you own every day—even if only for 20 seconds.

- The number of equities you are able to know well determines the maximum number of positions you should own. Remember their costs, know their present stops, and be able to picture their charts in your mind's eye.

Ask yourself:

- How would you grade your discipline in monitoring your positions?

- Did you lose focus while playing the waiting game? Become distracted during a vacation?

- Did you make excuses for missing market movements or procrastinating?

- Have you been completely frank in your self-evaluations?

- Do you enjoy this? Is it fun (at least for four days out of five)?

Stage 9: Selling

Although we used fundamentals when buying, price action should be the only determinant of what you sell and how quickly you pyramid out of a position. The financial markets have their own gravity, and that gravity forces prices to fall approximately three times faster than they rise. Your pyramid selling strategy should reflect this fact. While perhaps you entered into your position in tiered increments of 25, 30, and 45 percent, your exit should be nearly the reverse. Sell your position instead in tiers of 50, 35, and 15 percent. These percentages are not set in stone, but they should serve as a guide for your personal pyramiding levels. Your percentages should be determined by current market behavior at the time of the trade. As a rule, formulate your selling strategy before you ever buy an equity. The sisters strategy again plays a significant role in determining your exit points.

Until you develop a personal selling methodology, use simple triggers, such as moving-average downturns or the three-peaks system, to initiate a sell order and protect your profits.

Remain active in your stops adjustments, setting them just below points of previous support—those price points at which buyers historically moved in to support an equity. As an uptrend develops, don't forget to move your stops upward. Maintain a simple matrix of your most recent stops, and set alerts and triggers with your broker so you will be notified when they are hit.

Finally, remember that for each additional signal the market sends you, it will extract an ever-increasing cost in the form of a lower sale price. Information will cost you. Finally, don't make the mistake of thinking inaction is an acceptable choice. Deciding to do nothing is in itself a decision.

Remember to:

- Not let sudden success inflate your opinion of yourself and disrupt your trading rules.

- Accept being wrong, but never accept staying wrong.

Ask yourself:

- Did you freeze up on any investments? Can you determine exactly why?

- How will you prevent this kind of inaction from happening again?

- What is your personal uncle point? Do you logically understand this point? Has your risk tolerance changed?

- Do you enjoy studying the market's history and its past cycles?

- What three insights have you acquired about selling in the past year?

- Does your personal selling checklist need adjustment? Is it too simple? Too complex?

Stage 10: Revisit, Retune, Refine

After thoroughly recording your investment history and observations in your trading journal, reviewing your insights and the lessons you learned brings substantial payoffs. Taking the time to revisit each and every aspect of your trading plan with brutal honesty will help you improve and enhance your profits. Lessons are always more clear after some time has passed, once there is an emotional distance between you and a trade. Be candid with yourself as you evaluate your trade executions, methodology, and strategies. For this process to work, you must be humble and honest in your appraisals and willing to make a sincere commitment to improve. The market has an uncanny ability to humble those who are unwilling to humble themselves.

Remember to:

- Be humble and honest in your personal appraisals. Make a sincere commitment to improve.

Ask yourself:

- Looking at all your hits and misses, what changes should you make, on both a macro and micro level?

- Are you able to implement these changes? If not, why?

- What elements do your winners have in common? How can you replicate them more often?

- Do your losers display any consistent patterns? How can you purge those attributes?

Did you regularly deviate from your written trading plan? If so, should it be rewritten? It is striking how well you can do by modeling yourself after other highly successful people, adopting their attitudes and mimicking their behaviors. As an investor, this concept is shockingly effective. Fortunately for us, many such expert players are widely quoted and published, and they are constantly revealing key insights into their investing secrets. From Warren Buffett to William O'Neill, and Jesse Livermore to Richard Wyckoff, the stories, words, and opinions of famous traders are an unmatched source of priceless, hard-earned lessons and wise observations. Read about these investors. Act like these investors. You will be surprised at how lucrative the simple act of imitation can be.

What these world-class minds so often reveal is the struggle that accompanies success. Most investors fall off course and fail because they are determined to avoid pain while gaining only pleasure in the here and now. Without exception, the most successful traders are those willing to accept some short-term pain in exchange for greater pleasure and long-term gains. It is this forward-looking perspective that breeds consistently profitable trading—not a narrow outlook focused only on the present.

Personal Data Mining

Today's brokerage houses, such as Charles Schwab, Fidelity, and TD Ameritrade, likely know more about most individual investors and their trading habits than those investors know themselves. They have complex algorithms and unimaginable computing power that allows them to sift through a vast sea of raw consumer data to ascertain the exact details of your investment history. This alone should justify in your mind why Stage 10—revisiting, retuning, and refining—is so crucial. If your brokerage house is willing to spend millions to understand exactly how you trade, then you too should allocate some portion of your energy toward this activity.

These billion-dollar firms have learned to mine your life for data and understand you—and your investment actions in particular—in ways that you could never hope to understand yourself. Understanding your behavior in this way brings immense profits for these firms, so imagine the profits you yourself can glean from it. Luckily, your own self-awareness requires none of the complex data-mining algorithms these firms rely on. In place of intricate computer software, your trader's journal is your personal data-mining tool—and an exceptionally powerful one at that. If you stay disciplined in your journaling routines and frequently review the history and lessons it offers, your journal will provide a wealth of invaluable feedback about your investor self of yesterday, which will strengthen and improve your investor self of tomorrow. The fact is that our past quickly becomes cluttered with distorted memories, but a written trading journal captures them in the moment, preventing altered perceptions from interfering with the truth.

As investors, we must always strive to trade in the present. The tough reality, however, is that we often operate in the shadows of our past. These are the shadows we must mine, so to speak, in order to bring more light to our present trading. It is our behavior as investors that largely determines our successes and failures, not our brains or the technical tools we use. By carefully documenting these behaviors in a permanent, written format—your trading journal—you can learn from them honestly and productively.

■ The Investor's Big Three

Without exception, there are three unavoidably important personal elements all successful investors must balance: motivation, confidence, and action.

First, investors need the motivation to seek out meaningful investment tools and accumulate real market knowledge. Second, they must have the confidence to dig into complex investing methodologies and explore their own investor self. And third, they must embrace a personal action plan that converts their accumulated knowledge and self-awareness into bankable experience. As we near the end of this final stage in the Tensile Trading roadmap, we will explore each of these in turn.

Motivation

I challenge you to think seriously about your investing potential—not in terms of where you are today but rather where you could be tomorrow. Academic curiosity on its own will not grow your assets; you must be motivated enough to put your shoulder into it and build real-world investing experiences.

Here, I pose to you three important questions: How do you plan to get motivated? How do you intend to stay motivated? And how do you resolve to get remotivated when obstacles stand in your way? Answering these questions and uncovering your individual sources of motivation will determine the degree to which your future investment endeavors succeed and you meet your aspirations. The motivation to achieve success cannot come from someone else. It must emanate from your own determination to become a consistently successful investor.

Confidence

A number of recent academic studies have found that as many as one in every three Americans wrestles with insecurity. These individuals allow mountains of uncertainty, fear, and doubt to rob them of their confidence. This has ramifications in the individual investing arena as in every other aspect of their lives, and those ramifications can exact a steep financial toll. As you know, I believe it is essential for successful investors to write out and maintain a detailed investment plan. Even if you do not count yourself among the insecure, having a structured plan in hand brings an invaluable and unmatched sense of purpose and self-assurance to your investing. Whether your plan is focused on protecting your assets or growing your capital, it should explicitly set forth those investing tools and parameters that will help you reach your goals successfully.

Confidence is all about your vision for yourself and becoming the investor you know you can be. The old adage "you become the company you keep" has been validated by academics ad infinitum. If you have the confidence to spend your time with other smart and enterprising individuals, their assured demeanor will rub off on you. As a result, you must be willing to upgrade your relationships and become a talent hunter. Search out other successful investors, and pay attention to the wisdom they share with you.

Years ago, I set out to surround myself with a circle of smart and talented investors. I extended invitations to a group of first-tier traders and organized them to meet on a monthly basis. The group is not an investment club per se; that is, we are not pooling money to manage together. Instead, we meet to share our expertise, our passion, and our insights as a group with the purpose of expanding and deepening our collective investing knowledge. For my own trading, this group experience has provided a wonderful boost. Investing can be a lonely endeavor if you let it, and the best antidote is to surround yourself with talented individuals who share your interest.

Action

Over the years, I have met some highly motivated investors who ooze confidence on the outside but are still unable to pull the trigger when push comes to shove. For a variety of complex personal reasons, these investors are incapable of applying their sense of self-worth or converting their vast investment wisdom into profitable trading. In the stock market, knowledge is the new currency. And while it has immense value—just like a stack of cash—it cannot work its magic if you keep it tucked away in your pocket. It is only when you take out your wallet and act on the knowledge you possess that you can actually unlock the value of that currency.

At a seminar I attended, I listened to a talk by motivational expert Les Brown, who said, "If you do what is easy, your life will be hard. If you do what is hard, life will be easy." I find that this simple, yet profound statement encapsulates all that is required to achieve true mastery of the stock market. It is not enough to just take action. What is more important is to take those actions that are difficult or counterintuitive—those trades average investors so often shy away from. As an old college coach of mine used to say, "The key is to work smarter, not harder."

I know a very successful investor who once told me that her most profitable trades over the years were those that went against the herd. These were investments she made while wholly ignoring her broker's advice, instead basing her decisions on her own personal analysis. She knew how to follow her methodology and apply the currency that was her knowledge. It is easy to listen to the pundits on CNBC and simply follow their advice for the day. It is harder, however, to utilize your investment tool kit and follow your own personally relevant methodology.

The actions you take today are often predetermined by the actions you have taken in your past. If you have always followed the easy road, you may not be inclined to veer off it now or at other critical junctures in the future. Consider therefore that what you do today will in fact create a very likely forecast for your success—or lack thereof—tomorrow. Today's actions are the foundation upon which you build your potential to achieve great things. As such, it is not enough to simply ask yourself what you will choose to do today. Instead, ask yourself this: "How will the choices I make today shape the choices I am able to make tomorrow?"

▪ Thoughts on Transformation

The evolution from a novice investor to a self-disciplined, expert trader is an exceptionally transformative journey. Throughout my time in the markets, I have come to learn that it is not some complex methodology with magical tools or indicators that drives peak investing performance. Instead, for me, it is a manageable simplicity that helps maximize performance, one I achieve by pruning excess complexity from my trading system. As is my habit, I revisit each trade in detail and squeeze it thoroughly for every important lesson and insight it can offer. This process provides a steady stream of investing milestones that chronicle my journey of self-discovery. My core skills as a trader have been steadily developed in this very manner, with the market's behavior and my response to it continually showing me how to improve my future by analyzing my past.

As human beings, we have complex personal lives with needs that cry out and must be satisfied. The markets have taught me that I must address the daily realities of my portfolio before I deal with these personal matters. Separating and compartmentalizing these two distinct arenas in my life allows me to function most effectively in both areas. I trade as an individual, true, but I always feel that I am a part of a greater investing community, each of us practicing our collective craft. This assortment of individuals pushes and challenges me to become a better trader each day. Even while trading on my own, I am perpetually tuned into the broader community of investors, sharing ideas at every turn and using them to shape the trader I have become.

In the process of learning to sift through the massive amounts of complex information and data surrounding the financial markets, I have opened myself up to learning and implementing new ideas. With a firm sense of discipline, I manage to organize and employ the essential facts, to be persuaded by the truthful movements of my charts, and to act upon the conclusions this system offers. The rest of my personal life, after the markets close each day, is often a breeze in comparison.

I have accepted the fact that I have to run to keep up with the markets, not walk along at a meandering pace. Over time, I have remained energized, maintained a brisk jogging speed, and discovered that I have been able to outpace the majority of other individual investors. Much to my surprise, my performance has bettered even that of many high-powered mutual funds. The markets have taught me to put aside my ego along with my preconceived notions about how the market could and should be acting. I have learned to avoid defending a trade with emotions when the charts are deteriorating in front of my eyes. When the market speaks, I try to listen and act on what it says without my personal filters interrupting.

Trading the markets as a full-time independent investor, I have been able to operate by and for myself, free from the baggage of clients or employees. This experience has shown me that solitude can be both surprisingly enlightening and powerfully invigorating. What I have discovered about myself—much as you will discover things about yourself as you move onward in your investing journey—is that I thrive when faced with a steep learning curve. In a world that all too often accepts poor quality and tragically rewards mediocre effort, it is stimulating to be nurtured by markets that call the average and ordinary to account. I am reminded each day that you cannot accomplish anything significant by coasting, whether in trading the markets or living a full and enriching life.

My parting thought to you: Trade well; trade with discipline!

REVISIT, RETUNE, REFINE

Key Takeaways

- After every trade, it is important to review your decision making, evaluate your execution, and revisit your trading system to improve your probabilities of future success. After a losing trade, these are difficult tasks to perform, but it is those very moments that separate the successful investors from the average ones. By approaching this period of reflection with brutal self-honesty, humbleness, and a desire to improve, you will turn any mistakes that you have made into opportunities for growth.
- I like to categorize elements of my trading execution as either technical or emotional and recommend you do the same. This helps us to enhance our investor self so we can progress through the five levels of investor growth.

- As you already know, your investor self is dynamic and always changing. That is why it is crucial to regularly revisit *every* stage of the Tensile Trading program, reevaluating your progress and adjusting your written trading plan and rules accordingly. To achieve success in this regard takes motivation, confidence, and action—what I like to call the investor's big three.
- The Tensile Trading program, just like the markets, is cyclical. This positive feedback loop and process of revisiting, reviewing, and refining is an immensely powerful tool for success. With discipline, tenacity, and commitment to your financial goals, the road to consistent, high-probability, profitable investing is clear.

Tensile Trading is accompanied by a companion website at www.wiley.com/go/tensiletrading (password roze16). There you will find the following:

- Related links and helpful resources to augment *Tensile Trading*.

- Preview of the Tensile Trading ChartPack, a comprehensive organizational framework to help shape your market analysis, asset allocation, and portfolio management efforts, all in one convenient, carefully organized collection of over 90 ChartLists and more than 1,000 preformatted individual charts.

- Access to *Traders Journal*, the authors' weekly investment blog, which draws upon the material in *Tensile Trading* as it relates to the personal ongoing investing activities of the authors and the current market environment.

- Access to www.StockMarketMastery.com, the authors' personal investment education website where you will find up-to-date information on their latest seminars, investment courses, educational tools, and more.

Note: Page references in *italics* refer to figures.

Printed in the USA
CPSIA information can be obtained
at www.ICGtesting.com
LVHW080032291023
762031LV00003B/3